THE INFLUENCE OF JOHN MASON NEALE

JOHN MASON NEALE
1818—1866

THE INFLUENCE OF
JOHN MASON NEALE

A. G. LOUGH

LONDON

S·P·C·K

1962

First published in 1962
by S.P.C.K.
Holy Trinity Church
Marylebone Road
London N.W.1

Made and printed in Great Britain by
William Clowes and Sons, Limited
London and Beccles

The substance of this study has been
approved by the University of London
for the degree of Doctor of Philosophy.

This book is dedicated to the Glory of God, for my wife and children, and for the members and associates of the Society of St Margaret, in gratitude to my mother and in affectionate memory of my father, who took me on my first visit to East Grinstead.

Contents

Acknowledgements

The author gratefully acknowledges his debt to the following: a Sister of the Society of St Margaret, who helped greatly in the writing of this book by her prayers and encouragement; the Reverend Mother Superior of St Margaret's Convent, East Grinstead, for the loan of books and MSS., and for permission to quote from *St Margaret's Magazine*; the Reverend Mother Superior of St Saviour's Priory, Haggerston, for the loan of books and MSS.; the Reverend Mother Superior of St Margaret's Convent, Boston, Massachusetts, U.S.A., for permission to quote from *St Margaret's Quarterly*; Mrs Janet K. Lawson for the loan of MSS.; Dr F. Brittain for the loan of books and MSS.; the Librarian of Exeter Cathedral Library for the loan of volumes of *The Ecclesiologist*; the Librarian of Devon County Library for assistance in obtaining rare books from other libraries; the Superintendent of the Reading Room, British Museum, for access to books and MSS.; Longmans, Green & Co. Ltd for permission to quote from *John Mason Neale, A Memoir* (E. A. Towle) and *Letters of John Mason Neale* (M. S. Lawson); Hodder & Stoughton Ltd for permission to quote from *Collected Hymns Sequences and Carols of John Mason Neale*; the Proprietors of *Hymns Ancient and Modern* for permission to quote from their *Historical Edition of Hymns A. & M.* (1909); Faber & Faber Ltd for permission to quote from *The Architectural Setting of Anglican Worship* (Addleshaw and Etchells); The Faith Press Ltd for permission to quote from *The Religious Communities of the Church of England* (A. T. Cameron); A. R. Mowbray & Co. Ltd for permission to quote from *Memories of a Sister of St Saviour's Priory*; The Bodley Head Ltd for permission to quote from *Nathaniel Woodard: A Memoir of His Life* (Sir John Otter); Heath Cranton Ltd for permission to quote from *The Book of the Beresford Hopes* (H. W. & I. Law); the publishing staff of the S.P.C.K. for suggestions and guidance.

I

A Prophet without Honour

A RECENT writer has described John Mason Neale as "perhaps the most brilliant and versatile priest of the Church of England in the nineteenth century".[1] The late Canon Ollard wrote: "Some men come late into their own, and such has certainly been the fate of this most remarkable and gifted scholar. Neale died in 1866, yet forty years passed before his life was fully written (in 1906), and his *Letters* (an even more valuable contribution to his story) were only published in 1910. In his brief lifetime (he died before he was fifty) Neale was certainly a prophet without honour."[2] The object of this study is to substantiate these judgements, and to show something of the influence of this now little-known priest on the Anglican Communion.

Unfortunately there has never been a really satisfactory biography of Neale. The best account of his life and work is contained in a series of articles which appeared in *St Margaret's Magazine* (the magazine of St Margaret's Convent, East Grinstead), 1887–95. These articles, written by Sister Miriam, have been bound together in one volume.[3] In 1906 the Life referred to above, *John Mason Neale, A Memoir*, by Eleanor A. Towle, was published. This was sponsored by Neale's daughters, and was

[1] Peter F. Anson, *The Call of the Cloister* (1955), p. 337.
[2] Article in *The Treasury* (Feb. 1915), p. 482, entitled "Neale's Hymns and Sequences", S. L. Ollard.
[3] The title of this one volume (cited as *Memoir*) is *John Mason Neale, A Memoir* (this is not to be confused with Mrs Towle's book, which has the same title and will be cited as Towle, *Memoir*). Unfortunately the page numbers in this volume are not consecutive. In quoting from it I have used the following method for referring to pages in the footnotes. The first section, pp. 1–364, is quoted normally. For the following sections I have added the letters a, b, c, d to the number of the page to indicate in which part of the volume the page occurs, e.g. p. 1b is at the beginning of the third section and will be found near the middle of the volume; p. 1d is the beginning of the last section and will be found near the end of the volume.

intended to be a full biography. His daughters, however, were very disappointed with it when it appeared, considering it to be very jejune and inadequate in view of the material which was available. Because of this the eldest surviving daughter, Mary Sackville Lawson, decided to make a selection of her father's letters. These letters were published in 1910 under the title of *Letters of John Mason Neale*. The only other substantial book about him and his work was published in 1914, entitled *Collected Hymns, Sequences and Carols of John Mason Neale*. This collection was edited by the same daughter, Mrs Lawson. There is evidence from some unpublished correspondence that Mrs Lawson hoped that the late Canon Ollard would undertake a further biography of her father, but this did not come about. Thus the main sources for the life and work of Neale are the four books mentioned. Neale, however, was a prolific writer himself. Apart from the many books he wrote, he contributed numerous articles to journals, magazines, and newspapers. In his own writings there is abundant material for assessing his work and influence.

John Mason Neale was born on 24 January 1818, at Lamb's Conduit Street, Holborn. His father was Cornelius Neale and his mother before marriage was Susannah Good. The latter was the eldest daughter of Dr John Mason Good, a distinguished physician, writer, and linguist. Cornelius had a brilliant career at Cambridge, and evidently had ideas of entering the ministry of the Church, but owing to some scruples he did not receive holy orders until he was thirty-three. He died at the age of thirty-four, leaving a widow with four children: John Mason, five years old, Susanna, Cornelia, and Elizabeth.

After his father's death John Mason was put under the tutorship of the Reverend William Russell at Shepperton. From there he went to a school at Blackheath, thence to Sherborne for a year or two, and finally to Farnham. In 1836 he went into residence at Trinity College, Cambridge. Here, or perhaps earlier, he made his first acquaintance with the Oxford Tracts. With his friend Benjamin Webb and others he founded the Cambridge Camden Society. Though one of the most brilliant classical scholars of his year, he did not obtain classical honours, because he had no taste for mathematics, and in those days candidates for the Classical Tripos had to take mathematical honours first.

He was made deacon in 1841 with a title to the chaplaincy of

Downing College, Cambridge, but this chaplaincy was not very congenial to him and he resigned after a few months. For a short time he was assistant curate at St Nicholas', Guildford. He was ordained priest in May 1842, at St Margaret's, Westminster, by Bishop Monk of Gloucester and Bristol. The following day he was offered the living of Crawley, Sussex. He took up residence in the parish, but after a few months his health broke down and he had to resign. He was never instituted. At this time he married Sarah Webster, the daughter of the Reverend Thomas Webster of St Botolph's, Cambridge, and sister of the wife of his friend, the Reverend E. J. Boyce. On account of his health he had to spend the next three winters in Madeira. This change seems to have been beneficial to him, but he was never very strong.

In 1846 Neale was offered and accepted the wardenship of Sackville College, East Grinstead, a seventeenth-century almshouse of the Earl of Dorset. Here he remained for twenty years—the rest of his life. During most of the time he was unjustly inhibited by the Bishop of Chichester (an account of the proceedings will be found in Chapter 12 of this book). It is good to know that in the end the bishop withdrew his inhibition.

Neale's greatest work at East Grinstead was the founding of the Society of St Margaret. Besides this, he was a voluminous writer. In the introduction to the Sackville College sermons we read:

> His unresting pen pours forth work upon work, with marvellous rapidity, learning and versatility. Church History, theological essays, children's hymns and stories and catechizings, newspaper articles, Seatonian prize poems, translations into and out of Greek and Latin, pamphlets on questions of the day, Scripture commentary, historical tales, biographies, *cantilenae* in dog Latin, travels and College sermons. It was not a very unusual thing with him, to have sixteen of these various matters on hand at once. Still less unusual to put them all aside for the sake of telling a story to a child, or releasing a mouse out of its trap.[1]

Mother Kate, one of the early St Margaret sisters, writes of him:

> Into this place some time in the early forties, John Mason Neale was instituted as Warden of Sackville College. Young, ardent, enthusiastic, large hearted, full of sympathy, a poet, a scholar, a student, and

---

[1] *Sermons Preached in Sackville College Chapel*, vol. i, pp. ixf.

to crown all, gifted with intense energy of purpose, never to our judgement did a man seem more utterly out of place than was this young Priest, in the midst of these surroundings. To our judgement it seems so, but God's ways are not as our ways. . . . And this highly wrought, highly gifted young man, seemingly utterly wasted and thrown away in this bucolic *entourage,* was to kindle a light, which, by God's grace, has shone far and wide.[1]

Neale had five children,[2] the last three being born at Sackville College. He died in 1866 at the comparatively young age of forty-eight. After his death the following tribute appeared in *The Ecclesiologist:*

He died worn out with incessant work at the early age of forty-eight, leaving behind him the reputation of being one of the most learned theologians, one of the most erudite scholars, one of the best linguists, one of the sweetest hymnodists, and perhaps the foremost liturgicist of his time. The versatility of his powers was astonishing; and it may be doubted if his capacity and his fondness for hard intellectual labour was ever exceeded. Gifted with an extraordinary retentive memory, an indefatigable student, and trained from early childhood in the habit of fluent and graceful composition, he became one of the most voluminous as well as accomplished writers of his generation. Indeed, there is scarcely any branch of literature in which he did not distinguish himself, while in some he has left behind him no rival and no successor.[3]

In this study we shall attempt to give an account of Neale's work and influence in four fields: Church Architecture, the Religious Life, Hymnology, and Reunion. His influence of course was not confined to these four subjects. He was a great liturgical scholar. Dr Dugmore points out that he introduced the word *liturgiology* to the English language in his *Essays on Liturgiology and Church History.*[4] He was a pioneer in the revival of Catholic ceremonial in the worship of the Church of England. He was a great expounder of the mystical interpretation of the Scriptures, as can be seen in his many volumes of sermons. He would probably have claimed himself that his greatest literary work was his *Commentary on the Psalms.* He started this work in Madeira in

[1] Mother Kate, *Memories of a Sister of St Saviour's Priory* (1903), p. 13.
[2] The names of the children were: Sarah Agnes, Cornelius Vincent, Mary Sackville, Katherine Ermenild (Superior of the Society of St. Margaret, East Grinstead, 1902–32) and Margaret Isabel. Neale's sister, Elizabeth, was Superior of the Community of the Holy Cross, now at Haywards Heath, 1857–96.,
[3] *The Ecclesiologist,* vol. xxvii (old series) = xxiv (new series), Oct. 1866, p. 265.
[4] C. W. Dugmore, *Ecclesiastical History No Soft Option* (1959), p. 15.

1843, and he was engaged upon it at different times all through his life. He never saw the completion of the work himself. It was finished for him by his friend, the Reverend R. F. Littledale (1833–90).

Neale was a born teacher. He wrote many books for children— history books, stories of the saints, and historical novels. They were widely read, and continued to be reprinted until the early part of the present century. Some of them were translated into German and Russian.[1] He was a great teacher of prayer and the spiritual life. This can be seen in his many sermons addressed to the Sisters of St Margaret. To give an adequate account of his work and influence in all these fields would take several volumes. We shall therefore confine this study to the four subjects stated above.[2]

---

[1] J. M. Neale, *Deeds of Faith* (2nd edn, 1860), p. x.

[2] The following facts relating to Neale are worthy of note:

1. A society called *The Ecclesiological Society* still exists with its headquarters in London. This is in direct descent from the Cambridge Camden Society. It still uses the seal designed by Pugin in 1844.

2. The Society of St Margaret, with its mother house at East Grinstead, Sussex, besides its own daughter houses in England, Africa, and Ceylon, has now four independent Affiliated Houses, one of which is in Scotland and another in the U.S.A.

3. A *John Mason Neale Society* exists in England at Cambridge, and there is a branch in Australia.

4. There are now stained-glass windows of J. M. Neale in Chichester Cathedral, East Grinstead Parish Church, and St Mary's, Wellingborough. The latter was designed by his godson, the late Sir Ninian Comper.

2

The Cambridge Camden Society

NEALE'S interest in church buildings went back to his childhood. As a schoolboy he would often take long walks visiting country churches. When he went up to Cambridge as an undergraduate he was to launch a society which was to have a profound effect on the Church of England, and indeed on the whole Anglican Communion. A full account of the origin of the Cambridge Camden Society has been given by his brother-in-law E. J. Boyce, at one time rector of Houghton, Stockbridge, Hampshire.[1] There is also some reference to it in the diary of Benjamin Webb.[2] The latter was one of Neale's greatest friends from his Cambridge days and a regular correspondent to the end of his life.

Neale and Boyce entered Trinity College in October 1836. They spent the long vacation of 1837 together at St Leonards, and embarked on an architectural study of all the churches in the neighbourhood. Tours of different counties and studies of the churches were continued in subsequent vacations. In October 1838 Benjamin Webb entered Trinity College. He too was interested in church architecture and the Catholic revival. An entry in his diary dated 3 March 1839 refers to the "founding of a High Church Club" with two fellow-students. On 15 March a larger society was formed including Neale. The name given to it was "The Ecclesialogical Society" (there seems to have been some disagreement in the early days about how this word should be spelt). This, however, was only the prelude to the formation of yet another society. On 9 May we have the following entry in Webb's diary:

[1] E. J. Boyce, *A Memorial of the Cambridge Camden Society* (1888).
[2] Benjamin Webb's Diary (Bodleian Library, Oxford).

Neale gave a wine party to Thomas, Lewthwaite, Lingham, Boyce, Colson and me. All joined the new society: Neale made President and I sec. and treasurer. Chose the name of Cambridge Camden Society. We drafted a Church Scheme and sent it to be printed.

So started a lifelong friendship and partnership in church matters between Neale and Webb. "Church Schemes" were forms upon which the architectural details of church buildings were entered. Thousands of these forms were later to be filled in by keen young members of the Society. At the beginning, however, there was opposition to this new society from some of the other students. Boyce writes:

There was a storm brewing, and the threat to start a counter society was circulated. It was under the excitement caused by the opposition of some, who, because they could not rule, wished to destroy the original little coterie of lovers of Church Architecture that the following steps were taken by Neale, Webb and Boyce. . . . They determined to try to secure a Head and an influential leader to the movement. . . . To this end, one night after ten o'clock, these three (carrying with them the Brass of William de Fulborne) waited on their tutor, Archdeacon Thorp, and laid the state of the case before him. They entreated him to come to the rescue, and they did not leave him until he had promised to call forthwith a Public Meeting to be held in one of the lecture rooms of Trinity College.[1]

At this meeting held in May 1839 the Cambridge Camden Society was formed. It was named after William Camden, the antiquary, who died in 1623, but it had no connection with the Camden Society, also named after him.[2] Boyce does not give the exact date of the meeting, but in Webb's diary the following entry occurs on 24 May: "C.C.S. Committee in Neale's rooms and then General Meeting. Above 84 present."

Boyce states that at this meeting the Venerable Thomas Thorp, M.A., Fellow and Tutor of Trinity College, Archdeacon and Chancellor of Bristol, became the President of the Society, "and continued to be so, until, I believe, he took up his permanent residence on his living of Kemerton".[3] One interesting feature

---

[1] Op. cit., p. 9.
[2] The Camden Society was founded in 1838 by a few antiquaries and archivists. Its object was "to perpetuate and render accessible whatever is valuable, but at present little known, amongst the materials for the civil, ecclesiastical or literary history of the United Kingdom". Over twelve hundred copies of its publications were issued yearly between 1840 and 1862. In 1897 the Society was amalgamated with the Royal Historical Society.
[3] Op. cit., p. 10.

of the early days of the Society is the readiness of Thomas Thorp, Fellow and Tutor, Archdeacon and Rector—evidently something of a pluralist—to sympathize with and to assist this enthusiastic group of undergraduates in their schemes and plans for the improvement of churches.

Boyce in an appendix to his *Memorial* gives the laws of the Society when it was first formed. They begin with a series of quotations from *An Homily for Repairing and Keeping Clean and Comely Adorning of Churches*:

> It is a sin and a shame to see so many churches so ruinous and so foully decayed, almost in every corner. If a man's private house wherein he dwelleth be decayed, he will never cease until it be restored up again. . . . How much more then ought the house of God, which we commonly call the church, to be sufficiently repaired in all places, and to be honourably adorned and garnished, and to be kept clean and sweet, to the comfort of the people that shall resort thereto? . . . He is highly pleased with all those that diligently go about to amend and restore such places as are appointed for the congregation of God's people to resort unto.[1]

The object of the Society is stated to be "to promote the study of Ecclesiastical Architecture and Antiquities, and the restoration of mutilated Architectural remains". Membership was confined to past and present members of the University. Meetings were to be fortnightly in term-time. Tours of churches were made by members all over the country, and "Church Schemes", giving full particulars of the architecture of the churches visited, were filled in. "Taking Churches" became the technical term for this exercise. "Camdenian Field Days" were arranged, on which surveys of local churches were made.

In 1841 the Society started a periodical called *The Ecclesiologist*. Boyce assigns the origin of this to Neale:

> It was in October 1841 that Neale paid a visit to Boyce, then Curate of Holy Road, Southampton. Naturally the C.C.S. became the chief object of conversation, and upon Boyce complaining that members of the Society, who had removed from the University, were left without any information of its doings, and suggesting that the Society ought to have its periodical, Neale (one of whose characteristics was a "blow and a word") wrote off at once to the President, and to Webb, and Young, and Paley, the Secretaries, mentioning the suggestion, giving the sketch of the design for a monthly publication, and proposing that the name should be "The Ecclesiologist".[2]

[1] Ibid., p. 36. [2] Ibid., pp. 10f.

The first number was published in November 1841, and, according to the report read at the annual meeting on 11 May 1842, the following subjects were defined as within the scope of the publication:

Church Building at home and in the Colonies: Church Restoration in England and abroad: the theory and practice of Ecclesiastical Architecture: the investigation of Church Antiquities: the connection of Architecture with Ritual: the science of Symbolism: the principles of Church Arrangement: Church Musick and all the Decorative Arts, which can be made subservient to Religion: the exposing and denouncing of glaring cases of Church Desecration: Criticisms upon Designs for and upon New Churches.[1]

The Society rapidly increased in membership. In the second year of its existence, however, it met with some opposition on account of some rather caustic criticism in *The Ecclesiologist* of certain designs of new churches and restorations of old ones. This caused the resignation of some members. But in spite of this temporary setback the Society soon recovered and extended its influence remarkably. In 1843 "there were connected with the C.C.S. as Patrons, or Hon. Members, 2 Archbishops, 16 Bishops, 31 Peers and M.P.s, 7 Deans and Chancellors of Dioceses, 21 Archdeacons and Rural Deans, 16 Architects, and over 700 ordinary members".[2]

Two years later, in 1845, the Society was reorganized and became "The Ecclesiological (Late Cambridge Camden) Society". This, according to Boyce, came about for two reasons. First of all some of the articles in *The Ecclesiologist* caused alarm, because they were expressive of extreme ritual and doctrine. In a footnote Boyce says: "The contributors to that periodical seemed to prefer blisters and bitters to poultices and syrups in their doctoring."[3] The result of this was that several important patrons withdrew from the Society, amongst them Dr Phillpotts, Bishop of Exeter, Dr Kaye, Bishop of Lincoln, and the Duke of Northumberland, Chancellor of the University. The second reason for the reorganization was that "the most numerous and influential Members of the Society (which in its infant state consisted for the most part of Undergraduates) at that time had ceased to be resident in the University: and were in the position of Church

---

[1] Ibid., p. 11. [2] Ibid., p. 10. [3] Ibid., p. 12.

Officers, Country Clergymen, Architects, Church Restorers, Church Builders etc., while of the influential Members of the University not many belonged to it. In reality the Society had become a National rather than a University Society."[1]

A result of the reorganization was that the Society ceased to be tied to the University. The Ecclesiologist continued to be published, but from January 1845 for a year and a half it was independent of the Society. It was however conducted by the same writers. Boyce says: "The tone, principle and object were identical with these volumes (i.e. the first three); the difference consisted in this, that the C.C.S. was in no way answerable for the new series."[2] In May 1846, however, the copyright of the periodical was restored to the Society, and it again became responsible for its publication. It continued to be published at first every two months, and latterly every three months. The final number came out in December 1868. It had existed for twenty-seven years. At the end of the final number the editor wrote: "The work has been to all concerned, in all respects a labour of love. If it is abandoned now it is because still higher duties claim the less divided attention of those who have conducted this Periodical from its commencement to its close."[3]

As we have seen, Neale was the prime mover in the founding of the Cambridge Camden Society. It was launched in his rooms at Trinity College. He was chairman of the original committee, with Boyce as treasurer and Webb and Codd as joint secretaries. Neale remained chairman from 1839 to 1843. He resigned the chairmanship in the latter year, as he spent the winters of 1843–5 in Madeira. From 1845 to 1849 he was joint secretary with Webb and others. Thus we may say that for the first ten years Neale's was the guiding hand in the policy and work of the Society. Even while he was in Madeira he kept in close touch with Webb over ecclesiological matters. He was responsible for the launching of The Ecclesiologist, and according to Boyce took the largest share in the production of the first three volumes.[4] It is interesting to note that The Ecclesiologist survived for only two years after Neale's death.

We conclude this chapter with Neale's own appraisal of the work of this Society:

[1] Ibid., p. 14. [3] Ibid., p. 17.
[2] Ibid., p. 16. [4] Ibid.

In the winter of 1838–9 the Ecclesiological movement began in our own Church. Like all great movements one cannot trace its actual rise. The first visible embodiments were the University Societies. . . . England from one end to the other was moved almost as one man. The founders of the Architectural Societies were astonished at their own success. "It was the Lord's doing, and it was marvellous in our eyes." Those who were engaged in the work can never forget their astonishment at the spread of their principles. How, for example at Cambridge, before the law was abrogated which imposed a fine on all members, who did not visit some specified Church within four miles of St Mary's weekly, the C.C.S. already numbered Associates in every county of the kingdom. A new science was springing up, and a new science demanded a new name. That name, Ecclesiology, was first heard in the English Church.[1]

In the course of his last illness Neale said: "It really had been very audacious on the part of a few young men at Cambridge to undertake the entire reform of Church Architecture, and to assume for their motto, 'Donec templa refeceris'. But the temples had been built."[2]

---

[1] *The Ecclesiologist* (old series), vol. v (Jan. 1846), p. 4.
[2] *Memoir*, p. 283. *Donec templa refeceris* is a quotation from Horace, *Odes*, iii. 6.

3

Ecclesiological Conditions

To understand what the Cambridge Camden Society accomplished it is necessary to realize something of the condition of the churches in this country, and the kind of worship offered in them, before it came into existence. The following description of a typical church and its worship is given by A. J. Beresford Hope. He was an early member of the Cambridge society and a friend of Neale, though not always on the best of terms with him. He was a Member of Parliament, and a very keen churchman. He built St Augustine's College, Canterbury, and also found the money for building All Saints' Church, Margaret Street, London. This description is found in a book by him entitled *Worship in the Church of England*:

I may as well attempt to describe the visible form in which the Church of England and its worship were first made palpable to my childish senses in the reign of George IV, and at an opulent and beautiful market town of Surrey [footnote—Dorking] not thirty miles from London, which is now accustomed to very different services. The building was a large, and had been a handsome, Gothic church, but of its interior the general parish saw very little, except the nave and aisles, for the chancel was cut off by a perfectly solid partition covered with the usual sacred writings and some strange painting, among which Moses and Aaron shone with peculiar uncouthness. The eastern portion of the aisles was utilized for certain family pews or private boxes, raised aloft and approached by private doors and staircases; these belonged to the magnates of the neighbourhood, who were wont to bow their recognitions across the nave. There was also a decrepit western gallery for the band, and the ground floor was crammed with cranky pews of every shape. The pulpit stood against a pillar, with the reading desk and clerk's box underneath. The portion of the Communion office preceding the sermon, was, Sunday after Sunday, read from the desk, separated from the litany on the one side and from the sermon on the other by such a rendering of Tate and Brady as the unruly gang of volunteers with fiddles and wind instruments in the gallery pleased to contribute. The clerk, in a brown Welsh wig, repeated the responses in a nasal twang, while the local rendering of "briefs, citations, and excommunications" including announcements by this worthy, after the Nicene Creed, of meetings at the town inn of the executors of a deceased Duke. The hopeful cubs of the clerk sprawled behind him in the desk, and the backhanders intended to reduce them to order resounded against the boards. During the sermon this zealous servant of the sanctuary would take up his broom and sweep out the middle alley in order to save himself the fatigue of a weekday visit.[1]

This way of worship was normal throughout the Church of England at this time. But there were even worse examples in some places. Neale whilst on a tour of churches in 1842 encountered the following: "I must tell you a thing practised in Tong Church. The Squire has built a pew in the Chancel; when the Commandments are begun, a servant regularly enters at the Chancel door with the luncheon tray."[2] There were many examples of this kind of slovenliness and lack of reverence in the conduct of services in the early part of the nineteenth century.

In addition to this there was an extreme carelessness about the fabric and the furnishings of the churches. Many of them were in a neglected and sometimes dilapidated condition. The early volumes of *The Ecclesiologist,* from which we shall quote freely, give abundant evidence of this. The following description of the fine old Norman church of St Nicholas, Old Shoreham, Sussex, by Neale, was undoubtedly typical of many churches at that time. This church, we are told, was originally cruciform with north and south chapels to the chancel:

The two chapels had been destroyed long before the memory of man. . . . The east window was destroyed, and two nondescript lights with circular heads were inserted in its place; a window on the north was blocked by a modern monument, but to supply sufficient light a square hole was cut in the wall, which, being unglazed, was in wet weather plugged up with a corresponding piece of wood, a cheap and original invention. The north transept was in ruins, and separated from the church by an erection of brick so contrived as to conceal half the beautiful arch leading to it. The arcades of the tower were nearly concealed by the coating of rough cast with

[1] Quoted in H. W. and Irene Law, *The Book of the Beresford Hopes* (1925), p. 131.
[2] *Letters of John Mason Neale* (ed. M. S. Lawson, 1910), p. 33. This work will be cited as *Letters.*

which they had been loaded; the circular perforations under the eaves were, from the action of the weather, almost ruinous. . . . The nave was filled by pews of all sorts and sizes; the walls were reeking with moisture; every moulding had been clogged with plaster or whitewash; the pulpit had at first stood on the north side of the chancel arch, and the abacus had been knocked away to make room for it; it had been removed to the southern side, and the same accommodation had been made for it there; the Norman door in the transept had been blocked and was now half concealed by the earth piled against it: and a door opened opposite it faced with brick. The damp earthy smell which pervaded the building, the green mould which hung on the walls, and the broken uneven state of the pavement would have led the visitor to imagine that he was descending into the dungeon of a criminal, rather than going up to the house of the Lord.[1]

It is a good thing to know that under the guidance of Neale this church was later restored.

As another example of neglect we may cite the church at Kingstone-by-sea, Sussex. The north aisle of this church, which was "blocked off some fifty years ago remains in a disgraceful state of desecration, being used when we last saw it as a potato store".[2] In a letter to Benjamin Webb about this Neale says: "This I cannot stand—I only learnt it today—and tomorrow I am going to blow up furiously. If with no success, then I shall, all well, apply to Hare."[3] Hare was then Archdeacon of Lewes.

Even cathedral churches were not immune from this general neglect. The following is a description of parts of Canterbury Cathedral in 1844:

A beautiful stair-case turret to the south-east transept is entirely out of repair; and generally in this part the windows are broken, or their cills are vegetating with weeds. St Anselm's chapel especially requires the glazier. . . . The northern side, which is concealed very much by buildings, is even deficient in rain water pipes, and the walls are streaked with green. The most valuable sculptures are here unheeded. . . . The chapter-house is in disorder, damp and littered, and looks as if it were of no use in the modern economy of the Cathedral. The cloisters are a lumber-place for ladders, tackle, and stone, in spite of the noble efforts lately made (as we understand) in its favour by one of the canons. How unlike its former appearance, when it was used for devout meditation, its windows glazed, and its walls

---

[1] *Transactions* of the Cambridge Camden Society, May 1839. See also *The Ecclesiologist* (old series), vol. i (Nov. 1841), p. 12.
[2] *The Ecclesiologist* (old series), vol. i (April 1842), p. 100.
[3] *Letters*, p. 24.

painted with holy texts. The state of the crypt would not suggest to anyone that it is the resting place of some of the most illustrious primates of the English Church.[1]

Of the high altar it is said:

Ecclesiastical feeling is wanting, and while the altar in this glorious choir is a mean table with modern hangings, it is useless to expect much care and correctness elsewhere.

The internal arrangements of churches were usually most unsatisfactory and far from being conducive to worship. A picture in one of the early numbers of *The Ecclesiologist* shows a so-called proprietary chapel in a fashionable watering-place, with the pulpit and reading desk standing out from the east wall immediately above the altar. The chapel is not named, but the picture shows how ludicrous this kind of arrangement was.[2]

Pews, or pues, to use the spelling preferred by Neale, also known as "pens" in *The Ecclesiologist,* were a feature of most churches at this time. They were of the high box type, sometimes of all different shapes and sizes, and fitted with doors. The modern type of bench pew is referred to in *The Ecclesiologist* as "open seating". As we shall see later, Neale made a scathing attack on pews in the early numbers of this periodical, and one of his first published works was *The History of Pues*. We shall consider this pamphlet in our next chapter. For the present we shall take a few examples of pews from *The Ecclesiologist*:

In Eastwell Church, Kent, there has just been happily destroyed a pen so remarkable as to deserve to have its memory perpetuated. It was surmounted all round, to the height of about two feet, with a stage of glass work provided with lattices to open or shut, according (we suppose) as the truths delivered might suit or displease "ears polite".[3]

In the parish church of High Wycombe a pew seems to have taken the place of the ancient rood:

Above the chancel arch . . . and entirely blocking a window placed over it, is a pen in the shape of a huge oriel window of black projecting into the church, belonging to the Carrington family. It is fitted up with *sash windows* (to let up or down as may be found convenient), carpets and rich sofas of the most somniferous character. This small

[1] *The Ecclesiologist* (old series), vol. iv (Jan. 1845), pp. 43f.
[2] Ibid., vol. i (Nov. 1841), p. 20.
[3] Ibid., vol. ii (Feb. 1843), p. 101.

chamber is groined in imitation of a fan roof, and would appear to be of the date of James I.[1]

Another example is the following:

In St Michael, Stanton Harcourt, Oxfordshire, is an enormous pen supported on pillars, about ten feet from the floor, and protected by a canopy very much like a flat wooden awning.[2]

Holcombe Rogus in Devon could boast a pen "twenty feet by twelve, and twelve feet high".[3]

In another place there is an amusing reference to a *presentation-pew*:

We have often heard of silk gowns, silver teapots, and even easy chairs, being presented by their congregations to popular incumbents; but we believe a *presentation-pew* is a novelty, a thing unheard and unthought of till last year. Yet this singular method of testifying regard and respect to their Rector has been devised, as we are informed by parties on the spot, by the parishioners of St Peter's, Cheese Hill, Winchester, where a pue, in obnoxious prolongation of a faculty gallery, has just been erected "as a testimonial of esteem for their Rector, and for the use of his family". The worst part of this business is that the testimonial blocks up part of the east and of the north window, and is placed so as almost to overhang the Altar.[4]

The squire's pew was often a very luxurious affair, as is shown by the following:

In Pluckley church, Kent, the south chancel is separated from the rest of the church by high parcloses, and is entered by a door from the outside. The whole is fitted up in the most luxurious manner: the floor is covered with a rich Brussels carpet, under which are spread a quantity of sacks to keep the feet warm and make it soft. The chairs are old-fashioned and high-backed, and have elegant crimson seats. The whole is fitted up like a modern fashionable drawing-room.[5]

It would seem that Exton, Rutlandshire, could even beat this:

At the east end of the north aisle, is a neat parlour, duly enclosed by curtained and tapestried wooden walls, so as completely to exclude observation, and entered by two separate doors. The size of this

[1] Ibid., vol. ii (April 1843), p. 139. A picture of this pew may be seen in Addleshaw and Etchells, *The Architectural Setting of Anglican Worship* (1948), facing p. 96.
[2] Ibid., vol. ii (Feb. 1843), p. 107.
[3] Ibid., vol. v (Jan. 1846), p. 28.
[4] Ibid., vol. ii (June 1843), p. 168.
[5] Ibid., vol. ii (Feb. 1843), p. 102.

parlour is twelve feet by fifteen; it is richly carpeted, and contains thirteen drawing-room chairs, and a mahogany table in the centre. On the north side is a stove with a fender and fire-irons. Two sides of this abode of secluded luxury are flanked by stupendous monuments of white marble, in the revived or pseudo-pagan style, which serve to remind the visitor he is in a church, should he happen to forget the fact by the un-church-like character of this place.[1]

The kind of opposition which was met by those who ventured to challenge the rights of pew owners is shown by the following:

The Vicar of Tuxford "proposes to throw open all the pues, and make them common property". A placard has been posted up in the place calling upon "Protestants of Tuxford" to arise and defend their sacred rights: "Your country", they say, "has long been menaced by the intrigues of popery, but now your own sanctuary is polluted by popish superstitions; your seats, to which yourselves and ancestors have liberally contributed, are now to be wrested from you by Jesuitical intolerance!"[2]

Many churches at this time were being disfigured by extremely ugly stoves, which were coming into use. In the latter half of the nineteenth century the heating of churches had become a problem, though up to 1863 at least there was no heating system at all even in Westminster Abbey.[3] Stoves, however, were gradually being introduced into churches. The earlier numbers of *The Ecclesiologist* contain various attacks on them because of their ugliness. From all accounts many of them must have been great monstrosities. Neale himself was strongly opposed to them. The following are examples of what was happening:

The fine church of Totness [*sic*] is of the age of Bishop Lacey, as are also the stone Roodscreen and Pulpit, and very beautiful they are, but miserably disfigured. The Pulpit has an enormous capping of wood overlaying it, and it is choked by surrounding pens. The magnificent Roodscreen is surmounted by a strange congeries of high unsightly boxes, which are approached by a long flight of straight stairs formed in the Chancel. The Chancel is further ornamented by a large Arnott stove, fixed in the centre, the flue of which, after rising vertically to the level of the officiating Priest's head, takes a horizontal direction across his face, and escapes by a hole cut in the glass of the north window.[4]

[1] Ibid., vol. ii (Feb. 1843), p. 102.
[2] Ibid., vol. ii (Feb. 1843), p. 101.
[3] J. Bromley, *The Man of Ten Talents* (1959), pp. 143 f.
[4] *The Ecclesiologist* (old series), vol. ii (April 1843), p. 142.

In the church of Great St Mary, Bradley, Suffolk, is a flying stove, which for absurdity and ugliness can hardly be surpassed by anything of the kind in the kingdom. This sable machine is raised on two cast-iron legs, seven feet in height, and supported on a wooden shelf. It stands against the south wall, and people climb up to it by a ladder. A flue-pipe is carried out of the roof. We have been assured that to see this aerial engine steaming, smoking and hissing is almost irresistibly ludicrous.[1]

In another church in Devon a stove stood in the place of the altar:

In SS. Peter and Paul, Holsworthy, all the windows and window arches, with one exception have been removed, and sash windows and round arches substituted in red brick; the East end of the chancel is divided from the church and called a vestry; the East window is blocked, and in place of the altar stands a stove; on the outside a brick chimney assumes the holy symbol of the Saving Passion.[2]

In an article entitled "The Warming of Churches", we have the following:

Chimneys of red brick are recklessly built across richly traceried windows, along roofs, up towers through cement gable crosses. Iron flues peer through the roofs of naves and aisles; they are thrust through walls and windows; they are suspended from chains aloft, supported on legs below; pursue serpentine, zigzag, rectangular, vertical, horizontal courses among the pues and about the galleries; stifle the sickly, scorch the strong, amuse the irreverent, and distract and unutterably disgust all who have the least sense of catholic propriety. Patent chunks, Arnold's self-consumers of smoke; stoves with flues aerial, flues subterranean, and no flues at all; flying stoves, concealed stoves, hot-water works; every variety may be seen in our unhappy churches.[3]

Neither were cathedral churches immune from desecration through stoves:

An enormous black stove has been set up in the very middle of the choir of Bristol Cathedral, with a black chimney mounting straight up to the vaulted roof, which has actually been broken through to make a passage for it.[4]

It is convenient at this point to mention the Society's recommendations on the problem of heating churches. They are found in the article entitled "The Warming of Churches", to which

[1] Ibid., vol. iii (Sept. 1843), p. 64.　　[3] Ibid., vol. iii (Aug. 1844), p. 136.
[2] Ibid., vol. iii (Feb. 1844), p. 94.　　[4] Ibid., vol. v (Mar. 1846), p. 127.

reference has already been made, and in a pamphlet published by the Society under the title *Church Enlargement and Church Arrangement*.[1] There is little doubt that both express Neale's ideas.

In the former it is suggested that if artificial heat is really necessary, open braziers filled with coke and placed on the floor of the nave and chancel might be used circumspectly. "The brazier should be circular or octagonal, pierced and ornamented with some ecclesiastical pattern." It should only be used on the coldest days. "It may be lighted an hour or two before the service, and afterwards extinguished, by which sufficient heat will have been generated to warm the congregation during the time they remain in church." The article concludes: "But the simplest, the best, the most Christianlike method of warming a church is *to open it for Daily Prayers*. The effect caused by this means in producing warmth and dryness is so astonishing as to appear scarcely credible to those who have experienced it."

The pamphlet mentioned above does not refer to braziers. It recommends that church doors and windows should be shut tightly in service-time, and that at other times, except on very wet days, they should always be left open to let in the drying air. Pews, which prevent a free circulation of air, should be removed. But let the church be crowded twice a day for daily service, and this will make for warmth. Incense is recommended for drying and warming the air. Reference is made to the former use of the pomander, "a vessel in the shape of a silver apple full of hot water, which enabled the officiating priest in bitter weather to warm his hands, that he might be able to grasp the chalice securely". In conclusion it is said: "Our ancestors were more self-denying than we are; they did not go to church to be comfortable, but to pray."

Nobody would think to-day that the suggestion of keeping churches warm through daily prayer was a very practicable one. But the recommendation that doors and windows should be kept open in dry weather (outside service time) is a sound one. It would help to keep churches dry, and it would remove that fusty smell which so often pervades churches where windows and doors are always kept shut.

---

[1] *Church Enlargement and Church Arrangement* (1843), a Cambridge Camden Society pamphlet.

We have made some reference to the lack of reverence in churches at this time. The following are a few further examples. First of all we quote from a letter written to *The Ecclesiologist* on the irreverence of parish clerks and sextons:

I have known a parish clerk place within the rails a common black bottle, with a corkscrew, perfectly unconscious that it would be at all indecorous for the Clergyman, when habited in his vestments and ministering at the altar, to stop during the Holy Communion service and draw the cork from the bottle, in order to pour wine into the flagon.[1]

There was often little or no respect for the altar:

The incumbent of a parish within four miles of Cambridge, upon recently entering the church to attend a parish meeting, found to his horror and indignation the persons *sitting round the altar* (within the rails), in conference on the business under discussion.[2]

In a letter Neale describes an experience in his first service at Crawley on the Sunday after he had been ordained priest:

But, in the middle of the service, judge of my horror, when the Churchwarden, wanting to open the east window, got up on the Altar! Really the Protestantism of the people with respect to that is dreadful; it all arises from having a short Chancel. People are forced from want of room to put down their hats within the rails.[3]

Not only parish churches, but cathedral churches also, were subjected to much irreverence:

There are in some cases pue-openers, who receive money for providing the strangers with seats; and we have ourselves been asked for fees demanded by the vergers themselves. The prebendal stalls, the decanal seat, nay, the episcopal throne itself is occupied by women. The doors are no sooner thrown open (alas, how many of us have seen this happen!) than a rush and scramble for seats take place. We remember on a late occasion seeing the archiepiscopal throne at Canterbury occupied in the morning by two females, and in the afternoon by two privates of Dragoons.[4]

The following is taken from a Cambridge Camden Society pamphlet by Benjamin Webb:

I have seen some tables that would not be thought good enough for a kitchen, and some which serve also as cupboards for books and

---

[1] *The Ecclesiologist* (old series), vol. ii (Jan. 1843), p. 76.
[2] Ibid., vol. ii (Jan 1843), p. 170.
[3] *Letters*, p. 37.
[4] *The Ecclesiologist* (old series), vol. ii (Oct. 1842), p. 34.

cushions: nay the Church chest itself is in one place used for the Eucharistick Table, and in another place the same thing serves for an Altar and a stove! . . . I wonder men are not ashamed to use the Holy Table for a tool-box or work-bench while repairs are going on; and it is nearly as bad to make it a place for hats and shawls to be thrown on by school children and others, or for a desk for the registering of Marriages and Baptisms.[1]

From the quotations above it would seem that the Cambridge Camden Society was faced with a tremendous task in trying to inculcate decent standards in the ordering of worship and in the restoration, design, and furnishing of churches. It could of course be argued that the picture of the general condition of churches which is given in *The Ecclesiologist* is an exaggerated one, and that the Cambridge Camdenians went out of their way to find the most dilapidated and irreverently kept churches, in order to make their case for reform stronger. But whether the picture is generally true or somewhat distorted, the fact remains that this Society was soon to transform the Church of England. In the next chapter we shall consider the aims of the Society, and what it succeeded in accomplishing. We may perhaps end this chapter appropriately by quoting from a set of satirical rules for church-wardens, which appeared in one of the numbers of *The Ecclesiologist*. Their title is *Rules for Churchwardens 1810*. There are fifteen of them, and they help to show what the church restorers of the mid-nineteenth century were up against:

1. Never let the roof of your church be too high, for it looks old fashioned ; nor covered with lead, for red tiles are decidedly cheaper . . . nor open in the interior, for a neat whitewashed ceiling looks more clean and snug, and hides from view the decay of timbers, which might otherwise be rather alarming.
2. Never allow too many windows to remain, for the congregation might catch cold. Straw mixed with mud is an excellent material for stuffing the tracery; but bricks and mortar are better for the lower part. It is advisable to knock out the mullions, lest some foolish churchwarden should wish to open them again. The east window should be boarded up to display the altar-screen to advantage. . . .
3. Fonts and stone coffins should be placed in the churchyard to hold rain-water. They also form convenient troughs for cattle. . . .
4. If your church has any screen, it may be sawn up to mend the old seats of the poor people in the aisles, if any remain, or to make scrapers for their feet. But it is to be hoped that all the principal

---

[1] *A Few Words to Churchwardens on Churches and Church Ornaments* (1842), a Cambridge Camden Society pamphlet, which went into at least fourteen editions.

inhabitants are accommodated with convenient and spacious pues in the best part of the church.

5. The communion table should be of deal, not too costly. Carving or other ornament is decidedly objectionable. A piece of old green baize should be thrown over it on Sundays. Three legs and a prop are sufficient to support it.

6. The village school should be held in the chancel, which should be well supplied with straw and deal forms. The teacher's chair may stand within the communion rails.

7. Disused chantries and chapels should be used for storing coals, or for dust, ropes, spades, old lumber etc. They may also be boarded off for vestries.

9. Venetian windows should be substituted for the old Gothick, where it is possible. Any remains of superstitious paintings or glass may be sold to the glazier, or (if considerable) to private collectors,

10. The pulpit must be lofty. . . . The pues may turn any or every way, or no way at all . . .

14. All brasses, fresco-paintings, carvings, crosses, and other rubbish, should be cleared away from the interior of the church. Recumbent effigies should have the heads, hands, and feet broken off, and sold for cattle medicine. The little boys may carve their names upon them, an amusement which will keep them very quiet during long sermons . . .

15. Generally, everything ancient is superstitious, and everything superstitious is popish, and everything popish ought to be annihilated forthwith. By adhering to this principle strictly, churches may easily be rendered more suitable than they are at present to pure Protestantism.[1]

Thus the promoters of *The Ecclesiologist* sought to improve conditions by ridiculing the low standards that prevailed in worship, architecture, and ecclesiastical art. In the next chapter we shall consider with what success they met.

[1] *The Ecclesiologist* (old series), vol. iv (Nov. 1845), pp. 275f.

4

The Triumph of the Church Restorers

IN the original constitution of the Cambridge Camden Society the object was stated to be "to promote the study of Ecclesiastical Architecture and Antiquities, and the restoration of mutilated remains".[1] The Society, however, under the influence of Neale soon developed along more definite lines. It was these more definite lines which caused some to resign their membership. In the early numbers of *The Ecclesiologist* the following three points are continually emphasized with regard to the arrangement of churches: (1) the importance of the chancel, (2) the evil of pews, (3) the proper position of the font. Reference is made to these three principles in a review of a book by the Lord Bishop of Down, Connor, and Dromore (Richard Mant) in *The Ecclesiologist*:

> We cannot but congratulate ourselves that so many of the principles, which we have always, amidst much opposition, held, e.g. the superior sanctity of the chancel, the wickedness of distinguishing in the house of God between the rich and poor, the nature and position of the font, have found an advocate in one who is so distinguished.[2]

We shall now consider these principles in detail.

THE IMPORTANCE OF THE CHANCEL

The following extract from an article entitled "Romanesque and Catholic Architecture" is typical, and shows the line taken by *The Ecclesiologist*:

> Our arguments for Chancels have been briefly these: the unvarying use of the Catholic Church until the sixteenth century; the necessity of such arrangement for the symbolism of the holy building; their

[1] E. J. Boyce, *A Memorial of the Cambridge Camden Society* (1888).
[2] *The Ecclesiologist* (old series), vol. iii (Sept. 1843), p. 15.

universal existence in our old churches; their *designed* retention when the Church was reformed; the evidence afforded by Visitation Articles of the care with which our great Bishops of the seventeenth century regarded them; their occurrence in the few churches built prior to the Revolution; and above all the Rubrick,—unrepealed through successive revisions, nay *restored* after a temporary domination of Calvinian influence—THE CHANCELS SHALL REMAIN AS THEY HAVE DONE IN TIMES PAST.[1]

In another place we have criticism of a publication by the Reverend J. L. Petit, who was regarded as something of a black sheep by orthodox ecclesiologists. He had written a book entitled *Church Architecture,* which adopted "a merely utilitarian view of the subject", and made no reference to "any higher standard than that of mere *taste* in church-building, which is treated as a matter of trade, convenience, caprice or arbitrary arrangement, instead of one that has ever involved and been influenced by the most unvarying and exalted principles". On the question of chancels, about which Mr Petit was very shaky, we have the following:

We have the *command* of the Rubrick distinctly on our side, and by this alone we may be content to stand or fall. It must ever be borne in mind that the Chancel is, after all, the great and marked feature of a church, as differing from a conventicle or any other building, which may be erected in the same style. Now if we give up our Chancels, how can we hope to maintain the dignity of ecclesiastical architecture? How shall we succeed in making more square apartments much better than preaching houses? Again, it is the *omission,* not the *retention,* of Chancels, which is an innovation, and in these times sympathy and association with ancient forms conveys to the mind of the multitude a degree of reverence, which, it is to be feared, will hardly be imparted . . . by the bare fact of a building being consecrated and used as a church.[2]

By September 1844 readers of *The Ecclesiologist* had become so convinced about the necessity of chancels, that an article on "The Arrangement of Chancels" begins with the quotation of a typical inquiry:

What shall I do with my Chancel? You have convinced me by many and sound reasons that a long and spacious Chancel is an indispensable part of a church. I have such a Chancel: how shall I treat it?[3]

[1] Ibid., vol. ii (Oct. 1842), p. 12.
[2] Ibid., vol. ii (Feb. 1843), p. 112. See also Basil F. L. Clarke, *Church Builders of the Nineteenth Century* (1938), pp. 84f.
[3] Ibid., vol. iii (Sept. 1844), p. 161.

Thus the first principle of the Cambridge Camden Society was the importance and necessity of chancels.

THE EVIL OF PEWS

The attack on pews was opened by Neale in a paper read before the Society on 22 November 1841. This was later published as a pamphlet under the title *History of Pues,* and went into at least four editions.[1] Introducing his subject Neale writes:

> Pues have never yet found an historian. Nor need we wonder at this. For what is the History of Pues, but the history of the intrusion of human pride, and selfishness, and indolence into the worship of God? a painful tale of our downward progress from the reformation to the revolution: the view of a constant struggle to make Canterbury to approximate to Geneva, to assimilate the church to the conventicle. In all this contest, the introduction of pues, as trifling a thing as it may seem, has exercised no small influence for ill and an equally powerful effect for good would follow their extirpation. Hence it is that, from the first moment of our existence as a Society, we have declared an internecine war against them: that we have denounced them as eye-sores and heart-sores: that we have recommended their eradication, in spite of all objections, and at whatever expense: that we have never listened to a plea for the retention of one: for we know well, if we could not destroy them, they would destroy us.[2]

Neale shows that square pews did not exist before the Reformation. The universal custom of praying towards the east would have rendered them impossible. He assigns the introduction of pews to the early part of the seventeenth century. In the reign of James I, Convocation directed that "a convenient seat should be made for the minister to read service in".[3] This direction was the start of pews, "for when the clergyman had his, the squire, the franklin, the yeoman, each in their turn clamoured for theirs: and the evil came in like a flood".[4] Neale then gives evidence for the introduction of pews into various churches in the early seventeenth century; for example, "In 1620 St Mary-le-bow had square pews introduced into the Nave. This church is a peculiar

---

[1] *The Ecclesiologist* (new series), vol. iv (June 1847), p. 233.
[2] Neale, *History of Pues* (1842), pp. 3f.
[3] Ibid., p. 17.
[4] Ibid., p. 18.

of Canterbury, and Archbishop Abbot was no enemy to puritanical innovations."[1]

Pews were supported by Puritans and attacked by Churchmen. The Puritans liked pews because they could not be seen neglecting four ancient customs of the Church: (a) Bowing at the Name of Jesus; (b) Standing at the *Gloria Patri*; (c) Bowing towards the altar; (d) Kneeling for Communion—"Those who received the Holy Communion in their pues escaped the notice of everyone but the clergyman with respect to standing or kneeling ... and if the clergyman presented them, nothing was easier than to accuse him to the Commons of malignancy."[2]

Here Neale goes on to quote from "a curious tract written in 1641" by Ephraim Udall, D.D., against receiving the Holy Communion in pews:

The Communion is rent and divided into so many single societies of twos and threes as there be pewfulls in the whole church ... they can neither see nor hear until the minister come to the pews where they sit ... in which sometimes there are divers pews, and they far distant one from another ... and so to have the Minister to hunt up and down to search them out. ... It is a needless weariness to put upon the Ministers to go up and down the church reaching and stretching out, rending and tearing themselves in long pews, to hold forth the elements over four or five persons: it is also an occasion of shedding or spilling the bread and wine.

Neale comments on this: "From these extracts we may gather the opinion of a very 'low churchman' of his day on the great harm of pues."[3] He also goes on to remark that Sir Christopher

---

[1] Ibid., p. 20.
[2] Ibid., p. 40.
[3] Ibid., pp. 39–45. The full title of Dr Udall's tract was Τὸ Πρέπον Εὐχάριστικόν: *Communion Comeliness; wherein is discovered the conveniency of the people's drawing nigh to the Table in the sight thereof, when they receive the Lord's Supper. With the great unfitness of receiving it in Pewes in London, for the novelty of High and Close Pewes.* By Ephraim Udall, D.D., Rector of S. Austin's, London. In a footnote to this Neale writes: "In a copy of this Author's *Noli me tangere* in Trinity Library, is the following MS. note written in a very old hand: 'This pamphlet was written by Mr. E. Udall, Rector of S. Austin's. He was much followed and admired by the puritans before the rebellion, and esteemed a precious man among them. But when he perceived whither they were driving, he began to declare pretty freely against rebellion and sacrilege. He therefore published this and some other pamphlets to stop their career. But as they contained a great many insufferable truths, fit indeed to convict, but not to reclaim them, this stung them so severely that they resolved to be revenged on him, notwithstanding all his former moderation. They therefore not only deprived, but plundered him; turning his aged and lame wife out of doors, with particular circumstances of inhumanity and barbarity.'"

Wren made a gallant, though unsuccessful, stand against the introduction of pews into his London churches.[1]

It is worth quoting Neale's conclusions about pews at length:

I have shown you, that pues, originally the offspring of indolence and pride, were soon found most valuable assistants in defying Church laws. . . . I have told you that they were denounced by Laud, and Wren, and Montague and other holy Bishops, who, partly by their opposition to this very innovation, have won for themselves the Martyr's and the Confessor's Crown. I have not told you . . . the destruction and devastation which have followed pues into our churches. Roodscreens, once enshrining the chancel in their transparent net work, now cut down and baized into a pue-back; brasses once fondly viewed with the hope that they might preserve the name of a beloved friend for ever, now boarded over or broken in pieces; piers recklessly cut halfway through for the reception of a luxurious pue-corner; windows, fonts, sedilia, all bear witness against the innovation, for all have suffered by it. Nay, your Church, with every rubrick denouncing, and that in the strongest way, by implication, these abortions of a puritanick age, these distractors of devotion . . .which offend against our glorious belief in the Communion of Saints, she herself seems to urge you to lend your aid in the struggle now carrying on against them. . . . And we, who are called by our Ecclesiological pursuits to see more than others of these lidless boxes, painted every colour and all colours, these cattleless pens, therein inferior to the "pues in Smithfield", that they are never cleaned, but harbour in their tattered green baize the dust and corruption of a century: shall we not more than others exert ourselves to cast out the evil? Finally, be it remembered, that all objections against pues are *a fortiori* objections against galleries, which are *flying pues*.[2]

Galleries were almost as much anathema as pews, and it was through the work of the Society that they gradually came to be removed from churches. This fifty-page pamphlet ran into at least four editions, and was followed by a supplement.

It must be emphasized that one reason why Neale was so opposed to pews was because of his concern for the poor and underprivileged. In 1842 the Society published a leaflet entitled

[1] Neale evidently has in mind the following words of Sir Christopher Wren: "A Church should not be so fill'd with Pews, but that the Poor may have room enough to stand and sit in the Alleys, for to them equally is the Gospel preach'd. It were to be wish'd there were to be no Pews, but Benches; but there is no stemming the Tide of Profit, and the Advantage of Pew-keepers; especially too since by Pews, in the Chapels of Ease, the Minister is chiefly supported" (*Life and Work of Sir Christopher Wren, from the Parentalia or Memoirs of his son Christopher* [ed. E. J. Enthoven, 1903], p. 196).

[2] *History of Pues*, pp. 48ff.

Twenty-three Reasons for getting rid of Church Pews. Neale almost certainly had a hand in this. One of the reasons given is: "Because they were invented at first by people who thought themselves too good to pray by the side of their neighbours: and who were in those days too proud to join in the service of God with such as were poorer than themselves."

THE PROPER POSITION OF THE FONT

The earlier numbers of *The Ecclesiologist* have numerous references to the desecration of fonts. Often the old font had been removed from the church, used as a birdbath in some garden, and an unworthy new type of font substituted. The following are examples of the kind of thing that happened:

> The old Font belonging to the church at Tooting, Surrey, now stands as an ornament in a Clergyman's garden; "an elegant marble" basin having been placed *in the Chancel* instead.[1]

> When the old church of Mitcham, Surrey, was pulled down, and the present wretched fabrick erected in its place, the handsome Perpendicular Font was ejected, as not being smart enough, and found a resting place in the Patron's garden.[2]

> The Font at St George's, Hanover square, is unique in form and situation. It resembles a tolerably sized marble wine-cooler, fixed in a circular carved oak frame about a foot high. The whole machine runs upon castors, and is wheeled out when wanted from under the Communion-table![3]

> In St James, Bonsall, the font is disused, and a common blue bason on the altar substituted.[4]

A correspondent inquiring how to dispose of a modern font in the Grecian style is told that it should be broken up and buried forthwith. "The sooner it is concealed from the eyes of Christian men the better."[5]

Some of those, however, who had orthodox fonts did not even use them. Neale himself relates the following incident:

> A clergyman . . . was lately asked to take duty in a little parish about six miles from here (Stogumber, Somerset). When it was over there was a christening, and so he went to the Font and proceeded with

[1] *The Ecclesiologist* (old series), vol. ii (Oct. 1842), p. 32.
[2] Ibid., vol. ii (Jan. 1843), p. 79.
[3] Ibid., vol. ii (April 1843), p. 141.
[4] Ibid., vol. iv (Jan. 1845), p. 46.
[5] Ibid., vol. ii (June 1843), p. 171.

the service as usual. When he took the child in his arms, he found there was no water; he thought of course it was an accidental omission, and asked for some. The clerk was in astonishment; however, he sent for a glass of water, thinking the clergyman wanted it to drink. And, in conclusion, it came out that they never used it there![1]

The Cambridge Camden Society was successful in establishing these three principles in the arrangement of churches throughout the Church of England, and indeed throughout most of the Anglican Communion. Through constant propaganda the necessity of chancels came to be accepted; the box pews were gradually removed, and fonts were placed near the west door. On account of the work of Neale and his fellow ecclesiologists, churches were transformed, and a return was made to the medieval arrangement of a church. By far the majority of the churches of this country were of course originally designed for that arrangement.

It is interesting to note that Addleshaw and Etchells in their book on Anglican worship, whilst defending the box pews, admit that they had to go:

This method of seating, with so many pews in private hands occupying more than their fair share of the church and the frequent relegation of the poor to the background, had to disappear. As a method of seating it was incapable of finding room in our churches for the ever-growing population of early Victorian England, and became a positive hindrance to the Church's work. All honour is due to the churchmen who, under the inspiration of Dr Neale, introduced open seats into our churches.[2]

With reference to fonts the same book states that the ecclesiologists much disliked the practice of placing the font near the altar; and it is chiefly due to them that it is now so rarely found in that position.[3] In another place we read:

Few undergraduate societies have exercised such an influence. . . . The society revolutionized the whole appearance and arrangement of our churches: and there is hardly a building in any part of the world, belonging to the Anglican Communion, which does not betray the influence of its ideals.[4]

[1] *Letters*, p. 33.
[2] G. W. O. Addleshaw and Frederick Etchells, *The Architectural Setting of Anglican Worship*, p. 97.
[3] Ibid., p. 207.
[4] Ibid., pp. 203f.

This is a noteworthy acknowledgement from a book which for the most part does not approve of the church arrangements sponsored by the Cambridge Camden Society.

The influence of this Society was not confined to the three principles stated above. Further influence was exerted in the denunciation of vandalism in churches, the encouragement of the best in art and craftsmanship, and the insistence on the supremacy of Gothic architecture for church buildings, and the Decorated style as the nearest to perfection.

As an example of the attack on vandalism we have the following from an article on *Suggestions for Co-operation with the Objects of the Society*:

> Thousands of curious relics of antiquity yet lie in neglect and decay in village churches, merely because their use is not known, and therefore their value not appreciated. We well remember interfering with success for the preservation of a remarkably fine old carved oak pulpit. . . . At another time we happened to walk into a carpenter's shop just as he had sawn into several pieces a noble old rood-screen to make frames for newly painted tables of the commandments; and this because nobody in the parish could tell what its use had been. On another occasion we remember to have seen a large slice of exquisite Decorated tracery cut away from a Parclose, because (will it be credited?) its contiguity discomposed the capacious wig of the occupant of a neighbouring pew! who, however, very gravely promised to make up for his fault by giving the poor mutilated woodwork "a good jacket of blue paint next Michaelmas". Once we found a very good Altar-table of the seventeenth century ejected and its room supplied by an enormous rough iron-clasped chest! And once we discovered that an extremely curious pavement of ancient encaustic tiles had been remorselessly covered over with a new deal floor, because forsooth a lady could not logically comprehend a sermon while her feet were cold.[1]

Reference is made also to the following acts of vandalism:

> The Collegiate and Decanal Church of St Buryan possessed a very elaborate Rood-loft, mentioned in Lysons' *Cornwall*. This was cut to pieces a few years ago (not in the time of the present Dean), and among other base uses to which it was put, part was actually used in the reparation *of a pigstye*![2]

> We have heard from good authority of an instance of church desecration so shocking that we do not believe the like could occur *now*. Crediton church was formerly Collegiate, for twelve prebends;

---

[1] *The Ecclesiologist* (old series), vol. i (Jan. 1842), pp. 34f.
[2] Ibid., vol. ii (Nov. 1842), p. 62.

in process of time they were replaced by twelve governors, farmers and substantial yeomen of the parish. These functionaries used to dine together at stated times *in one of the chapels,* their wine etc. being kept in the church. A very large amount of church property was held by these men: but as they did not like, in winter, to be at the expense of purchasing firing, they hit on the plan of taking down from a magnificent open roof, the angels which served as corbels, cutting them up and burning them![1]

That the Cambridge Camden Society was concerned to encourage the best in art and craftsmanship, and to expose what was cheap and shoddy, is clear from many passages in *The Ecclesiologist* and from their pamphlets. In a pamphlet entitled *A Few Words to Church Builders* the following assertion is made: "The first great canon to be observed in church building is this: LET EVERY MATERIAL EMPLOYED BE REAL."

The following is taken from an article criticizing the design of a proposed new church in "a very populous part of Cambridge called New Town" (St Paul's):

A church which cost little need not be a cheap church, and a church which costs a great deal may be one. A cheap church is one that makes the greatest show for the least money. Now herein lies the fault of modern church builders. They *will* have the ornamental part of the church at whatever the cost of the church itself. . . . What need was there for a tower? . . . The chancel was necessary and the tower was not. . . . But if ornamental appendages are bad when anything real is given up for their sake, much more are they so, when they are imitations of that which they really are not. Stucco and paint, and composition, and graining, are not out of place in the theatre or the ball-room; but in God's house everything should be *real.* Plainness need not be inconsistent with reverence; pretence is, and must be. Our readers will see that we refer to the mouldings of the pier arches which are *cast in plaister*: to the pieces of wood in the roof, which appearing to be purlins and principals, have in fact little to do with its support; to the varnish which is intended to make deal look like oak; and other imitations of the same kind. Such a principle is what we refer to by the word cheap.[2]

In an article criticizing competition amongst architects the following advice is given to those who would design churches:

Remember the dignity of your profession, and scorn to disgrace it by entering into unworthy contests. . . . If you for your part reject competition, the system soon must fall, since increased architectural

---

[1] Ibid.
[2] Ibid., vol. i (Nov. 1841), p. 11.

knowledge will not much longer tolerate ignorant and faulty designs. Above all, if you intend to build *churches,* dismiss every mercenary or selfish thought, be content to labour as in God's service, without care for your personal fame, without thought of your personal sacrifices: strive in some degree to emulate your predecessors, whose names are perhaps lost to memory, though their works—works of faith—remain in unapproachable excellence and in imperishable glory.[1]

The Society of course emphasized the need to follow ancient models:

Any architect who would set the example of building new churches after the exact models of good ancient ones, would, we think, have the glory of commencing a new and happy era in the history of modern church-building. . . . Since church architecture in the present day is strictly imitative, why may we not copy whole and perfect edifices as well as detached and unconnected parts? . . . We should thus replace by new and perfect buildings the worn-out and mutilated edifices of our pious ancestors; and England might once again become the country, if not of glorious Cathedrals, at least of refined and chastened Christian art. Nor let it be thought that servile imitation implies a poverty of invention reproachful to our times. It is no sign of weakness to be content to copy acknowledged perfection; it is rather a sign of presumption to expect to rival it in any other way.[2]

Thus all that was best in art and craftsmanship was encouraged. The same applied to church music, which also came within the scope of the Society's work.

An incontrovertible canon of the Society was the supremacy of Gothic architecture over all other ecclesiastical architecture. Of Gothic it was claimed that the Decorated or Middle-pointed style was the highest. In one of the Society's early pamphlets, *A Few Words to Church Builders,* which in 1844 had run into three editions, we have the following:

We are not now called on to prove that *Gothic is the only Christian architecture.* We believe that after a well-fought battle, this point has been conceded, and that though secondrate architects may for a few years yet, employ Romanesque or revived Pagan, those who are at the head of their profession will be guilty of such errors no longer. . . . We wish however to restrict the choice of style still further than this. No one can sensibly employ Norman, and perhaps not judiciously even Perpendicular, when free to choose another

[1] Ibid., vol. i (April 1842), p. 83.
[2] Ibid., vol. i (June 1842), p. 134.

style. Early English, though it must perhaps be allowed occasionally should be used very sparingly. The Decorated or Edwardian style, that employed we mean between the years 1260 and 1360, is that to which only, except from some very peculiar circumstances, we ought to return. The reason for this is plain. During the so called Norman era, the Catholic Church was forming her architectural language; in the Tudor period she was unlearning it. What should we say of him, who wishing to acquire the elegance of a polished and expressive tongue should select models from a period, either before that tongue had escaped from barbarism, or after the process of over refinement had reduced it to a frivolous debility? Would not his failure be at once signal and unpitied? And why should an architectural copyist expect a different fate? Again the equilateral pitch and arch is the soul of Christian Architecture, shall we voluntarily give it up and try what we can to do without it?

Later on the same pamphlet refers to the development of Catholic art:

Once more it is agreed on all hands that the greatest glory which Christian Architecture has yet attained was reached in the early part of the Decorated style; the Art had followed the true clue till that period. . . . Now, if we really indulge the hope that there is yet a higher pitch of glory to be attained, and which future architects may hope to reach, we may well go back to that point where decay and debasement began . . . that we may thence strike out a more real and more faithful course; more real because Perpendicular employed meretricious enrichments, and *made* ornament for its own sake; more faithful, because the Tudor architects forgot their high vocation of setting forth truth by beauty, and symbolized worldly pomp instead of the Catholic Faith; instead of the teaching of the Church the promptings of Erastianism. . . . And if it be said that it is not adapted for a plain church, we reply, "*Nothing better!*" Its own exquisite grace renders it as perfect when unenriched as when more highly finished. This certainly cannot be said of Perpendicular; nor perhaps to the same degree of Early English. A large Perpendicular window, when stripped of stained glass has a glaring stare; a Decorated window never. A simple Decorated Church is only plain: a Perpendicular one of the same character is meagre and unsatisfactory.

The Decorated style, as the ideal of Christian architecture, was continually put forth in the pages of *The Ecclesiologist*. At the eighth annual meeting of the Cambridge Camden Society on 18 May 1847, in a debate on church restoration opened by A. J. Beresford Hope, Neale went so far as to say that he was ready to see Peterborough Cathedral pulled down if it could have been replaced by a Middle-pointed Cathedral as good of its sort. This extreme view, put forward no doubt mainly as a debating point, did not receive the support of the other members present, but it showed that with Neale there could be no compromise. The fourteenth-century Decorated or Middle-pointed style was the ideal. It was at this period that Gothic architecture had reached its peak. There had so far been no improvement on it. Therefore that was the style to be maintained for the present. In the course of debate, however, Neale agreed that if a better style was ever discovered, then Middle-pointed should make way for it.[1]

In the present century we have seen a revolt against Victorian Gothic architecture and the medievalism of the Cambridge ecclesiologists. Few people to-day would agree that Gothic is the only possible style of ecclesiastical architecture. Neale of course was carried away by his enthusiasm for the great achievements of the medieval builders.

To Addleshaw and Etchells "the period between the Reformation and the eighteen-forties", which to them is the classical period of Anglicanism, gives the best guide for the planning of churches for Anglican worship.[2] But Neale was not very interested in Anglicanism as such. To him the Church of England had no meaning apart from the rest of the Catholic Church, and should follow all that was best in the traditions of the whole Church.

Furthermore to Neale a church building should convey something of the mystery of God—what is nowadays called "a sense of the numinous". This could hardly have been true of the bare, whitewashed, pewed buildings of the eighteenth century. Addleshaw and Etchells indeed admit that the altar placed near to the people tends to detract from the numinous character of a building, but they assert: "It is surely the fact that the Church of England has definitely subordinated the 'numinous' or mysterious treatment of the altar to its close relationship to the faithful gathered round it for worship and communion."[3] To support this they appeal to the relevant rubrics in the Book of Common Prayer and to what they call "the basic Anglican documents". Neale, however, would have firmly refuted the view that the "period between the Reformation and the eighteen–forties" should be taken as a pattern for church architecture and the

[1] *The Ecclesiologist* (new series), vol. iv (June 1847), p. 238.
[2] Addleshaw and Etchells, op. cit., p. 225.
[3] Ibid., pp. 228f.

arrangement of churches. He would have made out a strong case for his own position by appealing to the first rubric in the Book of Common Prayer, which asserts so unequivocally: "*And the chancels shall remain as they have done in times past.*" Even if English was substituted for Latin at the Reformation, and the laity are to take their proper part in the church services, there is no authority in the Book of Common Prayer for altering the traditional arrangement of our churches. So Neale would have maintained.

It is also clear that Neale would have opposed the present demand for a central altar, which has come about through the modern Liturgical Movement. The Reverend Peter Hammond in a recent book, *Liturgy and Architecture* (1960), emphasizes that a church building must be a symbolic structure. "It must be informed from the outset by a theological understanding of its purpose." Neale would have entirely agreed with this. But what precisely is a church meant to symbolize? Here Neale would have differed from Mr Hammond. A church is meant to symbolize not simply the Church on earth, but the whole Church in this life and in the life to come. In a medieval church the chancel, with its rood screen adorned with paintings of the saints, symbolized heaven and the final destiny of the people of God. The chancel was the most vital and important part of the building. But the modern ecclesiologist would sweep all this away, and have a plain building with a central altar and no apparent mystery or reminder of the world to come. Such a church would appear to symbolize only the Church on earth, and leave out of account the great unseen Church in paradise and in heaven. It would seem that the world to-day, with its material outlook, above all needs to be reminded that this world is not the end and purpose of all existence but only a preparation for that which is to come. To Neale and his friends the traditional plan of a medieval church was a symbol of this great truth.[1]

Finally we may note the influence which the Cambridge Camden Society had on the Incorporated Church Building Society, or to give it its full title, the Incorporated Society for Promoting the Enlargement, Building, and Repairing of Churches and Chapels. This Society had been formed in 1818 with a view to providing new churches for the poor in the rapidly growing towns. In 1828

---

[1] For Neale's ideas about the symbolism of churches see *The Symbolism of Churches and Church Ornaments, by William Durandus*, Neale and Webb (1842).

the Society was incorporated. E. J. Boyce, in his *Memorial of the Cambridge Camden Society,* shows how the latter society completely changed the policy of the former in the matter of the enlargement and the building of churches. A memorial was addressed to the older society by the younger, and with great tact recommendations were made. The older society "received the Memorial with that respect which was due to its weight, and consented to re-consider and alter those *Instructions* to which strong objection was made". The result was that on 2 May 1842 amended *Suggestions and Instructions* were issued by the Incorporated Church Building Society, which met with the full approval of the Committee of the Cambridge Camden Society. They were said by this Committee to contain "an almost unexceptional guide to Church builders who may desire to erect new Churches in conformity with ancient usage, as to materials, construction and arrangement, and as throwing light on the views which have been advocated in *The Ecclesiologist* and other publications of the Cambridge Camden Society".[1]

Through the work, then, of this Society, during the latter half of the nineteenth century churches all over England were restored and new churches built. It would be true to say that there was hardly a church in the country which was not affected in some way by the Cambridge Camden Society. It was the fashion in some quarters during the first few decades of the present century to decry the work of the Victorian church restorers and builders, and to accuse them of bad taste, sentimentality and fussiness. But we only have to consider what would have been the fate of many of our ancient churches without the work of this Society, and the various Diocesan Architectural Societies which it encouraged, to realize how much it achieved. But for the ecclesiologists many of our ancient churches would have fallen into ruins. Moreover it is surely true to say that the Victorian restorations of old churches and designs for new ones would have been very much worse than they were, if there had been no ecclesiological movement. It is becoming recognized more and more that many of the Victorian churches have considerable artistic merit. Those churches which we condemn to-day as thoroughly bad in design were probably condemned with equal vigour in the pages of *The Ecclesiologist* at the time of their

[1] Boyce, op. cit., p. 21.

appearance. For the best designs we owe much to the Cambridge Camden Society. It set a high standard in ecclesiological matters.

In the early days such well-known London churches as St Paul's, Knightsbridge, St Michael's, Chester Square, and St John's, South Hackney, were criticized adversely in the pages of *The Ecclesiologist*. Out of thirty-one new churches in all parts of the country, which were reviewed in Volume III (Old Series) of this journal, eighteen were condemned, three described as mediocre, and only ten praised. Churches intended to be models were All Saints', Margaret Street, and St Mary Magdalene, Munster Square, both well-known London churches.

To give some idea of the extensive influence of the Society in its early days we conclude this chapter with a final quotation from Boyce:

> In order to show the widespread influence of the Cambridge Camden Society as early as the years 1842–3, it is sufficient to notice that in that year alone no less than 98 applications were made to the Committee for advice respecting the reparation of old churches, designs for new ones, details in connection with the internal arrangements of existing churches, designs for Church Plate and Ornaments. . . . In fact it may be said without exaggeration that not only from every part of the British Isles, but from almost every colony of the British Empire, applications for designs and for advice were received by the Committee almost every month without intermission.[1]

The man behind all this work was Neale.

Appendix

E. J. Boyce, in his *Memorial of the Cambridge Camden Society,* gives a list of the pamphlets published by the Society. They include the following:

1. *Church Schemes or Forms for the Classified Description of a Church*. These schemes were a special feature of the Society. Members visiting churches were expected to fill in all the architectural details.

---

[1] Ibid., pp. 22f.

The schemes were elaborated as the years went by. Boyce says: "The number of particulars mentioned in the first edition as requisite to be noted in a church was 58; in the second, 84; in the third, 113; in the fourth 236; and the seventh edition has 260."[1] He adds: "I have in my possession seventeen thin quarto volumes of the Schemes filled up by Neale, who was accompanied very often by Webb, Young, Codd, Thomas, myself and others, in his church visits; some of these consisting of the description of foreign churches in Holland, Portugal, Spain, Dalmatia etc."

2. *Hints on the Practical Study of Ecclesiastical Architecture and Antiquities.*

3. *A Few Words to Churchwardens on Churches and Church Ornaments: No. 1, For Country Parishes* (by J. M. Neale); *No. II, For Town Parishes* (by B. Webb). According to Boyce, "No. I was written in language to be comprehended by the most illiterate member of that body. 5000 of these tracts were sold within the space of six weeks, and the Committee of General Literature of the S.P.C.K. requested that the *Few Words* might be added to their list, which request was gladly granted."
This pamphlet went into at least fourteen editions.[2]

4. *A Few Words to Church Builders.*

5. *A Few Words to Parish Clerks and Sextons.*

6. *A Tract on Church Enlargement and Church Arrangement.*

7. *The History and Statistics of Pues, with a Supplement and a Flyleaf containing Twenty-four Reasons for getting rid of them.*

The Society sponsored many other publications, and even produced a simple contrivance for ascertaining the orientation of churches, which was called "The Orientator".

[1] Ibid., p. 28.
[2] *The Ecclesiologist* (new series), vol. iv, p. 233.

5

The Revival of Monasteries

IF Neale's greatest work at Cambridge was the founding of the Cambridge Camden Society, his outstanding work at East Grinstead was the founding of the Society of St Margaret. Of all his many works for the Church this was undoubtedly the closest to his heart. In a sermon to the Sisters on one occasion he said: "Were He to take me tonight, the part of my life, the dearest, happiest, and for which I am most thankful, would be that in which I have had to do with you." In another sermon he speaks of "the little oratory that I love best of any place in the world".[1] Gerard Moultrie in a short memoir of Dr Neale, published just after his death, wrote: "After going to a distance to preach or to lecture to large numbers, as he frequently did, he always said on his return that he had rather preach to his own Sisters in the dear little oratory than to all the world besides!"[2]

Before we consider this work, we must first see briefly the circumstances which led to the revival of the Religious Life in England. From the time of the Reformation until the nineteenth century there had been no religious orders in the Church of England. Quite early in the nineteenth century, however, we find the idea of sisterhoods being canvassed. In December 1825 an article appeared in *Blackwood's Magazine* which described the life and work of the Beguines in Belgium, and recommended that an order of Church of England nursing sisters for hospitals be established in this country:

> . . . let all serious Christians, I say, join, and found an order of women like the Sisters of Charity in Catholic countries; let them be

[1] *Sermons Preached in a Religious House* (1st series), vol. i (1869), p. 41, and (2nd series), vol. i (1874), p. 164.
[2] *Dr Neale* (reprinted from the *Churchman's Companion*, 1866), p. 8. This will be cited as *Dr Neale*.

selected for good plain sense, kindness of disposition, indefatigable industry, and deep piety: let them receive not a technical and scientific, but a practical medical education; for this purpose, let them be placed both as nurses and pupils in the hospitals of Edinburgh or London, or in the county hospitals.[1]

In 1826 the Reverend Alex R. C. Dallas, while curate of Wooburn, Buckinghamshire, drew attention to the lack of proper nursing facilities for the poor:

> The doctor often lived a great distance, and the care of a large circle of parishes was committed to one young practitioner. The village nurses were deplorably ignorant, and Mr Dallas having resided in France, and having seen the superior nursing and the many advantages resulting from the system there carried on of the "Soeurs de la Charité", devised a plan for the same system to be adopted in England.[2]

Dallas published a pamphlet entitled *Protestant Sisters of Charity,* which, according to A. T. Cameron, was circulated widely. This pamphlet was addressed to the Bishop of London (Howley), and it was suggested that the archbishops and bishops should be earnestly entreated to support the proposals for Sisters of Charity. Nothing came of these suggestions at the time in the Church of England, but the pamphlet inspired Elizabeth Fry, the Quaker philanthropist, to start a nursing establishment on the lines suggested in East London, at Raven Row, Whitechapel.

Another to recognize the need for Sisters of Charity in this country was the poet, Robert Southey (1774–1843). In his *Colloquies* he refers to them as follows:

> There is nothing Romish, nothing superstitious, nothing fanatical in such associations; nothing but what is righteous and holy; nothing but what properly belongs to that θρησκεία, that religious service which the Apostle James, the brother of our Lord, has told us is pure and undefiled before God and the Father. They who shall see such societies instituted and flourishing here may have better hope that it may please the Almighty to continue His manifold mercies to this Island, notwithstanding the errors which endanger it and the offences which cry to Heaven.[3]

These somewhat hesitant sallies in the early part of the nineteenth century, however, were not to develop into anything like

---

[1] Peter F. Anson, *The Call of the Cloister* (1955), pp. 25f.
[2] *Incidents in the Life and Ministry of the Revd. Alex. R. C. Dallas* (1873), quoted in A. T. Cameron, *Religious Communities of the Church of England* (1918), p. 10.
[3] Cameron, op. cit., p. 12; Anson, op. cit., pp. 26f.

a full campaign until the coming of the Oxford Movement. One definite fruit of the Catholic revival started by the Tractarians was the restoration of the Religious Life to the Church of England—revival made easier by the great need for practical works of mercy amongst the poor in England at that time. One reason why sisterhoods were able to make their way in the Church was the dire necessity for a ministry of devoted women amongst the poor and in the hospitals.[1] It was felt that this ministry could best be supplied through religious communities.

The type of nurse employed in hospitals and in the home was often most unsatisfactory. Writing in 1855 a Mrs Jameson gives the following account of an inquiry into the type of women employed as nurses at that time:

On the whole the testimony brought before us is sickening. Drunkenness, profligacy, violence of temper, horribly coarse and brutal language: these are common. We know there are admirable exceptions, more particularly in the great London hospitals. . . . Still the reverse of the picture is more generally true.[2]

If the nurses employed in hospitals were often of bad character, what of those employed to nurse the sick in their homes? A leaflet, entitled *St Margaret's House, Rotherfield*, dated 3 December 1855, most probably written by Neale himself, has the following about home nursing:

Every Parish Priest must have felt the want of nurses to whom he can with any degree of satisfaction entrust the charge of his sick poor. The general character of women, who alone are usually to be procured, is too well known. At the very time when sickness might dispose the sufferer to receive religious impressions, the behaviour of the attendant, in many instances, the only attendant, is such as effectually to put an end to all hopes of benefit derivable from the visits of the Clergyman. And the gross ignorance of village nurses has long been lamented by every parish doctor as interfering, oftentimes fatally, with the beneficial result of his remedies.

Thus religious communities for women came into existence partly as a result of the Catholic revival, but also because of the great need for nurses of character to look after the poor. Nursing sisterhoods were founded to meet this need. The heroic qualities shown by the early nursing sisters in various cholera epidemics

---

[1] Cameron, op. cit., p. 16.
[2] Ibid., p. 17.

in East London and Plymouth did more to commend the work of religious sisters than anything else.

Cameron shows something of the rapid growth of these sisterhoods:

> Once a start was made and the Community ideal attracted the attention of the Church, Sisterhoods began to be founded rapidly, and the period between 1845 and 1858 saw the rise of no less than twelve. They are as follows: Park Village, merged into the Society of the Holy Trinity, Devonport, 1845; Community of St Thomas the Martyr, Oxford, 1847; Nursing Sisters of St John the Divine, London, 1848; St Mary, Wantage, 1849; Society of the Holy Trinity, Oxford, 1849; St John Baptist, Clewer, 1852; St Margaret, East Grinstead, 1855; St Mary the Virgin, Brighton, 1855; All Hallows, Ditchingham, 1856; Holy Cross, 1857; St Peter, Horbury, 1858.[1]

This list shows how quickly sisterhoods began to grow in the middle of the nineteenth century. Once a light had been kindled the fire soon spread.

Both Sister Miriam and Mr Peter Anson suggest that the idea of founding a sisterhood first came to Neale when he was writing his book called *Annals of Virgin Saints*.[2] This was published in 1846. This assertion may be true, but there is evidence that Neale had definite ideas about the revival of the Religious Life in the Church of England at least three years before this. This is shown by his second novel, *Ayton Priory*, published in 1843, and written mostly whilst Neale was in Madeira. In a letter to Webb at this time Neale writes:

> My story has got on very much. I think you will like it. I dwell principally on three points—the curse of Abbey Lands, the Benefit, and the Possibility of Monasteries—contrasting them with other modes of giving vent to a devotional spirit.[3]

Neale deals fully with the question of the revival of the Religious Life in the preface of this novel and in the story itself. In the preface he states that there is hardly any subject which has recently occupied a larger share of the attention of churchmen than the possibility and expediency of a revival of the monastic system. "The following tale is intended, as well to set forth the

---

[1] Ibid., p. 40.
[2] *Memoir*, p. 306b, and *The Call of the Cloister* (1955), p. 339.
[3] *Letters*, p. 51.

advantages, and all but necessity of the re-introduction of monasteries, as to suggest certain practical details connected with their establishment and subsequent working." He fully realizes the prejudices against any such revival.

> So intimately are they [religious communities] in the minds of most, connected with the corruptions of Romanism, that it will be a matter of great difficulty to make the contrary clear. Though we may again and again quote the universal testimony of the early Church in favour of the monastick life, though monasteries abound in those Churches, which view Rome with as much dislike as does the most bigoted Protestant, though we may bring forward passages, in which Divines of all classes, in our own Church, have spoken of their re-introduction as a desirable thing, from Bramhall and Thorndike down to Latimer and Burnet, the prejudice against them will be as obstinate, the outcry as clamourous as ever.

He recognizes some of the problems which would arise, such as "the question of vows, and the connexion of religious houses with the parochial system, which must some day be settled". He wishes that "some more able hand" had undertaken the task, and he hopes he will not be "one of those injudicious advocates, who by their folly sometimes defeat or delay a scheme involving the interests, which they thought to serve".[1]

He goes on to give an account of the chief points made in the story:

1. The dissolution of the monasteries was a horrible crime. It was "forced on, not approved by the Church".

2. Sacrilege has always been regarded by the Church as one of the blackest sins, and the curse by which every religious foundation was guarded has followed the spoilers and their descendants.

3. Monasteries have from the earliest times existed in every branch of the Church, and are a great strength to the Church.

The possible advantages of monasteries are enumerated as follows:

> The blessing of intercessory prayer constantly made in them is incalculable: that the Church system, involving nightly as well as daily supplication, can nowhere else be fully acted out: that a body of men, deeply read in ecclesiastical history and controversy, and surrounded by an atmosphere of Church feeling, would be fostered in them, which would be ready to oppose any new attack of heresy or infidelity: that colleges cannot, in this respect, possess the same

---

[1] Neale, *Ayton Priory or The Restored Monastery* (1843), pp. iv, v.

advantages: that self-discipline could in religious houses be practised more regularly, and closer communion with God be more attainable: that they would be invaluable as abodes for young men between their leaving the University and entering on the care of souls, as supplying a course of training, intellectual, moral, and religious: that aged priests might be thus provided with an asylum, who now, though physically unequal to their duty, must either retain it, or be reduced to poverty: that important ecclesiastical works might here be undertaken with the advantage of uninterrupted opportunities and leisure hallowed by religion, and a division of labour: that an asylum would be furnished for such as were without friends, or, who in the decline of life, wished to devote all their time and thoughts to the preparation for their approaching change: that those, who are immersed in business, or otherwise entangled in worldly pursuits, might here, in such seasons as Lent and Advent, find a place of salutary retirement: that the diminution of personal and other expenses on the part of inmates would set free a large portion of wealth for the service of God: that the poor might be tended in them both spiritually and corporeally: education carried on upon strictly sound principles: funds for church-building amassed: and church artists trained in devotional as well as professional habits.[1]

This list of possible monastic good works is extremely comprehensive. Neale's imagination and enthusiasm evidently carried him away here. It would seem impracticable for any one community to engage on such a variety of good works at the same time. But the list shows that Neale saw all the possibilities.

We shall now consider the story itself. "Ayton Priory" was formerly a Cistercian house. It was bestowed by Henry VIII on Lord Cromwell, and the agent, whom he employed in turning the estate into money, "gloated over the treasure which the abbey church presented to his sacrilegious eyes". For three hundred years the Priory passed in rapid succession from one family to another. Misfortune and ruin came on all these families.

When the story opens the Priory has recently been bought by a Colonel Abberley. Sir John Morley, the local squire, who is a good churchman, has misgivings about some of his own property, which originally belonged to the Priory. He has a talk with his elder son, Robert, about this. He comes to the conclusion that he should repay the Church the sum of £16,160. His son agrees with this decision. It is later decided to build a new church at Ayton with the money.

[1] Ibid., pp. vi ff.

At about the same time Colonel Abberley's son, Charles, is rather unhappy about a picnic party being held in the ruins of the Priory by some of the local gentry. Sir John's action about his church property moves Colonel Abberley to consider his own position. The two gentlemen meet, and a discussion about the dissolution of the monasteries takes place. Sir John makes the point that the main fault of the medieval monastic system was that the monasteries were outside episcopal jurisdiction: "far from being the abodes of vice . . . the monasteries of the 16th century—and how much more of the earlier ages—were as pure, as holy, and as well fulfilling the purpose of their institution, as it were possible that they should be".[1] In defence of monasteries he argues: "But suppose that all the tales against the monasteries were true, was that any reason for suppressing them? The Church, as a Church, was far more corrupted than the monasteries, as monasteries; What then? Was She to be annihilated, or reformed?"[2]

Later, in chapter 8, Sir John, in a further discussion with Colonel Abberley, definitely advocates the revival of monasticism in the Church of England:

> Excepting in our own and daughter Churches, with perhaps the Indian, I do not think any other is without monasteries. In those Churches, which are in communion with Rome, everyone knows they are most numerous: but not less in the various members of the Eastern Church. Russia, for example, abounds with them; so does the patriarchate of Constantinople; so do those of Alexandria and Jerusalem. Now when we see other branches of the Church supplied with a set of religious houses set apart for the peculiar service of God, we cannot but feel it an undesirable peculiarity that we alone should have none such.[3]

Sir John goes on to state four advantages, which the revival of monasteries would bring to the Church:

1. They would be an aid to the missionary work of the Church in rural and industrial parishes.

> How many tracts of land, for instance, are there, where five or six cottages are scattered here and there on some vast savage common,

---

[1] Ibid., p. 80. It should be noted that this was written when Neale was a young man. What he wrote sixteen years later shows that he recognized that there were many corruptions in the later medieval monasteries. See *Sermons Preached in a Religious House* (second series), vol. ii, pp. 582f.

[2] Ibid., p. 81.

[3] Ibid., pp. 125f.

nominally belonging to a parish of which the church is three or four miles off. Now, in cases like these, of what inestimable benefit would a stationary body of priests, and deacons, and laymen qualified to act as readers, be found. . . . And perhaps it is still more exactly suited to those manufacturing districts where a town springs up in the course of ten years. If, when the first large works in such a place were set on foot, a small cell were placed near it, as an offshoot to some larger house; then as one house sprung up after another, and one row behind another, the priory church would be open to them. The brotherhood would attend them; and the Chartist, and Socialist, and Atheist would have less chance of spreading their deadly poison among them.[1]

2. The second advantage of monasteries is that they would be houses of learning:

It is evident that the active and laborious life of a parish priest does not allow him time, had he the means, of laying up much deep learning. He must be content with an influence over his immediate flock; for the Church at large, except in the ways of example and prayer, he can do little. He wants the extensive library, which he may consult. . . . If you run over the writings of our principal divines, you will see that the greatest of their works were written by those who were not . . . engaged in parish duty. Hooker's Polity is a glorious exception. . . . But when any new and dangerous heresy appears, when any great article of faith is called in question, when the voice of the earliest and purest age of the Church is to be consulted on any given subject, when our own branch of the Church is to be defended against whatever enemy; then there would be, if we had our monasteries, a race of men ready at once to spring up the champions of the Catholic Faith, trained, not by a few hours' study, but by the investigation of years to unravel the most subtle heresies, and to penetrate, as deeply as man may do, into the depths of Theology.[2]

3. The third advantage of monasticism would be the benefits of intercession:

Much of this is, I allow, applicable to the Daily Service as we actually have it: much more was applicable to it when the Hours were said six times, instead of twice, daily. But the beautiful system of nightly prayer, that can only find place in a monastic establishment. The Church then, not content with supplicating the blessing of God on Her children at all hours of the day, sends up Her petitions for them at a time when they are more peculiarly exposed to danger, and when they are unconscious of the safeguard of Her prayers.[3]

[1] Ibid., pp. 126ff.   [2] Ibid., pp. 132f.   [3] Ibid., p. 136.

4. The fourth advantage is that monastic houses could be used as asylums for orphaned clergy daughters, aged priests, and for retreats. Of the latter object it is said:

> Periodical retirement to such a house might be most salutary for one deeply engaged in business: an Advent or Lent so passed would be, as it were, a breathing time for the soul, an untwining of the close poisonous embrace of weekly affairs; a strict lesson in setting the affections on things above. This is often practised in foreign Churches; why should it not be in our own?[1]

All these four advantages of monastic houses are discussed at length in the story.

Later Colonel Abberley refers to the "undeniable fact, that our country as a country, has never flourished so much as it has done since the dissolution", and asks if that does not show that the dissolution was right. Sir John Morley (who of course is Neale's mouthpiece) replies:

> I am by no means prepared to admit that national prosperity is any criterion of God's favour to a nation. It is of course easy to collect a large quantity of passages from the Old Testament, which seem to prove that it is. But these . . . were especially addressed to a people living under an immediate Theocracy. . . . If the prosperity of nations is to be the measure of their goodness, who were ever more pious than the Lydians, Babylonians, and Romans? What people ever pleased God more than the Saracens and their successors? . . . No! the hypothesis will not hold; but if it did, your case would be by no means clear. True; England seems at the present time to be greater than ever: both in commercial enterprise, and in successful warfare, in talent, and industry, and wealth and glory. But is this all real? Is there not within her a deadly disease, which no remedies as yet administered have affected? Are not the conditions of the poor, and the rapid spread of atheistical and anarchical principles tokens of a downfall (unless God of his mercy interpose) sudden and fearful? Did not Niebuhr long since give it as his opinion . . . that England, like Rome under the emperors, was sinking slowly but surely by a decay, of which the cause could not be explained, and therefore for which no cure could be found? Your arguments cannot, indeed they cannot stand: we have "robbed God" and His Church: and while we hold the gains thus acquired, how can we pretend, as a nation, to make any freewill offering? Talk of our charities! Why, we are not paying the interest of the money seized at the Dissolution. Talk of our prospect for good! "Riches, unjustly gotten, shall not profit in the day of calamity."[2]

[1] Ibid., p. 137.   [2] Ibid., pp. 142ff.

In the course of the story Charles Abberley is a suitor for the hand of Catherine Morley (daughter of Sir John), but Sir John refuses his consent on the ground that no child of his shall ever enter into a family "living, like the Abberley's, on Church property".[1]

Charles Abberley, unsuccessful in his suit, retires to the quiet rectory of a college friend. Here he studies Spelman's "History of Sacrilege".[2] He comes to the conclusion that his family's property should be returned to the Church, and writes to his father about it. Colonel Abberley replies that he has not the slightest intention of parting with it. The letter never reaches his son, who has a bad accident whilst riding. Colonel Abberley is at Sir John's when the news of this accident arrives. He is much put out by the news, and he makes a vow in Sir John's presence that, if it shall please God to restore his son, he will give up his lands, or their purchase money, to God's service. For ten days Charles' life is in the balance. When his restoration to health becomes certain, Colonel Abberley consults Sir John about his vow. He asks his opinion about the re-establishment of monasteries. Sir John replies: "I not only think that it would be one of the greatest blessings which could be conferred on the English Church, but that it is one of those things which will, sooner or later, be done in some way or other. At the same time no one is more conscious than myself of the immense difficulties attending the design."[3]

Sir John then discusses the four most formidable problems: (1) Vows; (2) Authority; (3) Daily Services; (4) Discipline.

1. The question of vows is discussed at great length. The conclusion is that life vows in the present state of the Church are not possible. But a monastic establishment without some sort of vows is out of the question: "a monastery without vows would be little better than a religious hotel".[4] The best solution under existing conditions is considered to be to fix two limits to vows—three months and five years. At the end of five years they could of course be renewed.

2. Under the question of authority the whole organization of a religious house is considered. It seems that Neale's view was

[1] Ibid., p. 122.
[2] Ibid., pp. 169ff. Sir Henry Spelman's *History of Sacrilege* was first published in 1698. Neale and Haskoll produced a new edition in 1846.
[3] Ibid., p. 185.   [4] Ibid., p. 187f.

that such houses should be under the bishop. They should be small: a prior, or superior, with twelve brethren is suggested for a normal house. The building should consist of a chapel, a library, a hall or refectory, a general parlour, an infirmary, a lodge for the prior, a porter's lodge, and two cells for each of the brethren. One or two rooms for the reception of strangers, and cloisters, would be desirable. The house would be financed by the gifts of the richer brethren. Even the question of a salary is considered. It is reckoned that £300 or £400 per annum would be suitable for the superior. This very considerable sum was thought necessary, "because it would be highly desirable that he should be able, in case the interests of his own house, or of the Church required it, to take a journey for the purpose of obtaining information, consulting libraries, giving and receiving advice etc."[1] The brethren would each receive a small stipend for the purpose of clothing themselves. The dress would be the same for all, "probably that of our clergy, with the constant addition of cap and gown".

3. With regard to the daily services it is stated first of all that the superior and one of the brethren should be priests. There should also be a deacon.

At first the Daily Service of the Church would probably be all that the Bishop would authorize. He might, however, according to the Rubrick, allow the Litany to be said daily. Thus four services would be provided. Supposing that Matins were said daily at six a.m.; the Litany at nine; the Holy Communion administered at twelve; and Vespers said at six; what an angelical life would such a one be, compared with those which are now led; though, I confess, falling short of those advantages, which a more extensive ritual would supply. And probably, in time, a form of Compline might be authorized ... or perhaps the use of certain psalms at certain hours might be established by competent authority. . . . The chapel would be very small; but so far as it went, it should be perfect. . . . In an establishment of this kind, the re-introduction of copes would come almost naturally.[2]

Services would be choral, and there would be an organ. The chapel would always stand open for private prayer.

4. The final point dealt with is that of discipline. This would include the observance of fasts and vigils, and a rule of silence.

---

[1] Ibid., p. 192. [2] Ibid., pp. 193f.

"There would be no mixing in society at all without leave of the superior." Great authority would be placed in his hands. He alone would see newspapers and magazines, because it would be important for him to be acquainted with what was taking place in the Church. He would regulate the time of rising and retiring to rest and other details.[1]

It is suggested that any future monastic establishment should be independent of the parish priest, but directly under the bishop, who should nominate the superior. This opinion was expressed by Neale, of course, long before his experiences at Sackville College with the Bishop of Chichester. In the light of this later experience he might have modified the views expressed here:

> The old system, by which abbeys were exempted from episcopal jurisdiction, was totally indefensible: but, because we allow that, do not let us err too much on the other side. I would have the superior in all cases nominated by the Bishop, who should be *ex officio* visitor of the house, and therefore competent to remove its head in case of ill-conduct or lax discipline. But to make the parish priest another visitor, what is it but to introduce a new order of men into the Church?[2]

In the end Colonel Abberley is convinced by Sir John's arguments, and he asks how he may set about restoring Ayton Priory as a monastic establishment. We quote Sir John's reply in full, because it shows Neale's attitude towards bishops in his early days. When bishops later let him down, he—unlike Newman—never lost his faith in the Church of England and her power of revival. Sir John counsels writing to the bishop:

> Lay all your wishes before him: tell him what you will be able to settle on the institution, and request him to take the whole thing on his own hands. I think he will not say, nay. If he does, your duty as a Churchman is clear; to give up all further idea of the step, and to lay out the money from the sale of the abbey lands, (either keeping them in your own possession, or parting with them, as you please) to some other charitable use. If he consents to the plan, you, of course, must leave its details entirely to him.[3]

The story concludes with the wedding of Charles Abberley and Catherine Morley, and the consecration of the new church at Ayton. The bishop officiates at both. After the ceremonies, the

---

[1] Ibid., pp. 194f.   [2] Ibid., p. 196.   [3] Ibid., p. 202.

bishop, Colonel Abberley, and Sir John Morley retire to the latter's study, and the question of the restoration of Ayton Priory and its re-establishment as a monastery is discussed. The reader is left to imagine for himself the result of this important conference.

This book was Neale's second novel, written when he was only twenty-five. It shows how profoundly at this early age he had studied the subject, and how far he thought the revival of the monastic life a practical possibility in the Church of his day. He had no doubt that such a revival would come about. It was, however, another eleven years before he was able to put any of these theories into practice.

6

The Society of St Margaret

WE have seen that Neale had very definite ideas about the
revival of the Religious Life in the Church of England,
and the forms it might take, long before he had the
opportunity of putting any of his ideas into practice. This opportunity did not occur until some eight years after his arrival at East
Grinstead. That he had fully equipped himself theoretically for
founding a Sisterhood is clear from his sermons to the Sisters.
In a sermon preached in 1861 he says:

> I have read, my Sisters, the biographies of as many women, I suppose,
> who had entered the Religious Life as any English priest: before I
> had to do with you, from interest only, (which, I hope, means that
> God was leading me on to have the care of Sisters—ah! and I wish
> I had followed His lead better!) since then, from duty.[1]

In another sermon preached at Baldersby in 1863 on behalf of
the Sisterhood he says:

> Before its commencement, in the January of 1855, with four Sisters,
> three of whom still remain . . . I visited a great many Sisterhoods
> in France, principally the Sisters of St Vincent de Paul, the Little
> Sisters of the Poor, the Blue Sisters and the Beguines, to learn
> what they thought of the difficulty and possibility of such a work
> [i.e. the particular work of cottage nursing undertaken by the
> Sisters]. The answer was always the same: "It is the hardest that
> women can undertake; and *you* will find it impossible, because it
> requires an amount of Grace, which cannot be had out of the True
> Church; *we* succeed, not without great labour; but *you* must utterly
> fail, however well you mean, and however hard you try." As you
> may easily imagine, *that* prediction did not frighten us.[2]

Neale was thorough, to say the least, in any undertaking, and
his work with and for the Sisters, as we have seen, was the dearest

---

[1] *Sermons on Passages from the Prophets*, vol. ii, p. 82.
[2] A. M. Allchin, *The Silent Rebellion* (1958), p. 105.

to his heart. His own account of the beginning of the Society of St Margaret is given in a long letter to Benjamin Webb, dated 1 February 1855. Neale, of course, had been on very intimate terms with Webb since their Cambridge days, and in this letter he is quite unguarded in his reference to other parties:

You know that, five or six years ago, it was a favourite speculation of mine, how it would be possible ever to get at the scattered collections of houses in our great Sussex parishes, so as positively to evangelize them as you might do a heathen country, for they are heathen to all intents and purposes. Some three or four years ago Fowler had an idea that by nurses, trained physically and religiously, something might be done; he laid the subject before the Rural Deanery, every one was pleased with it, but nothing was effected. . . . After this I saw the incalculable good that was done at Horley by the daughter of a master-brickmaker, who had been partially trained at Oxford. . . . After that, but long before the Nightingale affair, I happened to know three persons—two ladies, one not— who were anxious, and to whom the way was open, to join a Sisterhood; but which? Then I saw the nucleus of what I wanted to do, if I could get co-operation. I first wrote to, or saw, the most *prononcés* of our friends . . . and they all were enthusiastic in favour of trying what we could do. Then (you know my abhorrence of the pseudo-asceticism at St Saviour's, Osnaburgh Street, and Devonport) I went to Clewer twice, and learnt all that I could there, and had a long correspondence with the Superior, who is one of the most sensible women I ever saw. Before I could do more, it was necessary for me to have a Superior for my future Sisterhood. Her I found in Miss Gream, the very exact person of all others that I could have chosen, just about the right age—forty-five; used all her life to parish work; used to nursing. . . . With the help of some of our friends I drew up some rules, based on those of Clewer, so far as the great difference of the design would permit. The scheme then resolved itself into this: to have a central house—at present *some-where*—hereafter, when we get a new Bishop, connected (if it can be so) with this Chapel, in which we may have a community of trained Sisters, ready to be sent out at the Superior's discretion *gratuitously* to any Parish Priest within a circuit of (say) twenty-five miles, that may need their services in nursing any of his people; he to be responsible, so far as may be, for their management, safety etc., while they are in his parish. In that circle from here we have about twenty villages and five towns, where they would be thankfully received at once. Now my little cub was beginning to take good proportions; the next thing was to feed him. Just then came the Scutari business. On this I took courage, and wrote to everyone in our part of the Diocese that had a chance of being in favour of the plan—high and dry, moderate, hardworking men etc. Then

I first learnt how completely I had hit the right nail on the head. I had not a *single* demurrer to the scheme, though in some cases my selection might almost have provoked it. Then I began to beg; and certainly I succeeded there quite beyond my hopes. The next thing was to find a firstrate, and yet morally respectable, hospital, where the Sisters might be trained. . . . First I tried the Sussex County Hospital, but, after some negotiations, that failed. At Westminster I succeeded. The House Committee at once passed a resolution granting those whom we may send admittance. . . . By this time I had a pretty certain prospect of seven or eight; but I wanted more. . . . The week after next, all well, we send the first to Westminster to be trained, and shall then hope to keep on with them. *When* there will be enough, or *what* will constitute enough, to make them into a Community I cannot yet say. All my copies of the rules are out, but as soon as I can get one I will send it to you. You know they are only as yet proposed, so any suggestions will be most acceptable. . . . I have printed a little statement of our scheme, simply speaking of nurses, "whether ladies or others", and dropping all name of a Sisterhood. This is to be sent to 210 parishes which lie in our district, not in my name, but in that of old Gream, who entered heartily in the plan. What the result of that will be remains to be seen. I have given you very little idea of the eagerness of co-operation I have met with; it is the greatest hit I have seen since the first start of the C.C.S. But you have little idea of the constant hard work and driving it takes; it requires one's shoulder to be always at the wheel—however, it goes. . . .[1]

We have quoted this letter at length, because it is Neale's own account of how he felt his way towards the formation of a nursing Sisterhood, and the first steps which he took in order to put his ideas into practice. We may note here, as with his earlier work for the removal of pews, his deep concern for the poor. As he looked out of his study window at Sackville College to Ashdown Forest and the surrounding country, he thought of the many remote cottages often with sick folk in them, and nobody to nurse them. It was the sufferings of the poor that impelled him to start this work. We may also note that, of the Sisterhoods formed in the nineteenth century, the Society of St Margaret was one of the first to be devoted in its active work primarily to the nursing of the poor in their homes. Other Sisterhoods started at this time were more concerned with penitentiaries, orphanages, and schools. The Community of St John Baptist, Clewer (founded in 1852), in its early stages was chiefly concerned with penitentiary work. Hence Neale refers in his letter to "the great difference of the

---

[1] *Letters*, pp. 233ff.

design" between his own proposed community and that of Clewer. Neale seems to have been one of the first, in these early days, to have his Sisters trained as nurses in a London hospital.

In the letter above Neale expresses his "abhorrence of the pseudo-asceticism of St Saviour's, Osnaburgh Street, and Devonport". It is rather difficult to understand his lack of sympathy with these two societies. The Sisterhood of the Holy Cross, which had been started by Dr Pusey and the Reverend William Dodsworth at Park Village West in 1845 in the latter's parish of Christ Church, Albany Street, London, had moved in 1852 to Osnaburgh Street, in the new neighbouring parish of St Mary Magdalene, Munster Square. The Society of the Most Holy Trinity had been founded by Miss Priscilla Lydia Sellon in 1848 with the approval of Bishop Phillpotts of Exeter, in the parish of St James, Devonport. Miss Sellon worked under the guidance of Dr Pusey, and the two societies became very closely linked. When Dodsworth seceded to Rome in 1850 and was followed by one of the Sisters, Dr Pusey felt that it would strengthen the Sisterhood of the Holy Cross if it was associated more closely with Miss Sellon's Society. By 1854 Miss Sellon had virtually become its Superior.[1] In view of the often violent protestant opposition to Sisterhoods at this time, one would have expected Neale to have made common cause with others who were working for similar ends. In fact Miss Sellon's concern for the sufferings of the poor must have been as profound as that of Neale. A year after the foundation of her Devonport society she was faced with a violent cholera epidemic in Plymouth, which she and her Sisters tackled with magnificent courage and competence. Neale evidently disapproved of her autocratic methods and the extreme asceticism which had been a mark of the Sisterhood of the Holy Cross in its early days.

It is related that during Lent 1851 one of these Sisters had only one meal a day, consisting of thick oatmeal, which was not taken until nine p.m. On Maundy Thursday she had some porridge at noon, and then fasted completely, not even taking water, until Easter Day. Ten days later she contracted gastric fever, and died shortly afterwards.[2] Neale did not approve of such extreme asceticism.

[1] Peter F. Anson, *The Call of the Cloister* (1955), p. 240.
[2] Ibid., pp. 237f.

At the end of the letter quoted above Neale refers to "the constant hard work and driving" which the formation of the Sisterhood involved. Supporters had to be found; postulants had to be investigated; a suitable house had to be procured; funds had to be raised. All this entailed numerous letters. On 1 December 1854 Neale wrote in his diary: "My first begging letters." On 4 December he was able to write: "Hunt sends £5 and promises £5 more for the S.Hd. This is the first money actually promised— God be thanked for it." The following is an unpublished letter written by him to the Dowager Countess Somers in London on 7 December 1854, and is no doubt typical of many others written at this time to possible benefactors:

I very much hope that I may be able to interest your ladyship in a plan which I have for some years had in my mind, and which now seems likely to be realized.

We are intending to establish a Sisterhood in this place, where you know there are great facilities for such a thing—the object of which will be best explained by my quoting the first of its proposed rules.

"The object of this Institution is the supplying to villages which lie within a distance of 25 miles of the locality in which it is situated, Sisters of Mercy; who, when requested by the clergyman of the parish, and under his direction, may visit and attend the sick, and do such other works of charity as hereafter may be found expedient or practicable; the numbers of, and means possessed by, the Sisterhood being duly taken into consideration."

Every one knows how much parish priests complain of the want of such assistance; and more especially in such a district as this, where the parishes are so extensive, and the country so wild. East Grinsted [sic] is a very central situation for this work. Within the prescribed limits there are five important towns—Reigate, Dorking, Cuckfield, Seaford, Shoreham—besides about 20 villages, and here, at first starting, the clergy would be glad of our help; and when our railway is open, which is to be in March, we shall have no difficulty in reaching any of them.

All the clergy within our limits, whom I have consulted with respect to the scheme, are in favour of it; some enthusiastically so. I hope that we shall find a sufficient number of persons willing to work; some we have already: but we stand sadly in need of funds. I know very well that zeal is the first requisite and strength the second; nevertheless we cannot avail ourselves of either without money. I want to raise at least £300 before the beginning of Lent, when I should like to commence. I am trying every one who is likely to be interested in the matter: and I cannot but hope you may feel disposed to assist us in setting on foot a scheme, which, if it succeeds, must be of so much benefit, and that not to our particular locality, but to so large an extent of country. Those who will be most benefited by it, the clergy, can, for the most part, only give their good wishes and advice; and if we are to be enabled to carry on the work, it must be by applying to those to whom God has given the means, as well as the will to help. Some of our poor people here have before now been very thankful for your ladyship's kindness, and that is one reason why I am the more encouraged to appeal to it again. . . .[1]

This letter met with a ready response, for on Christmas Eve Neale was able to write a letter of thanks. In this letter he adds that the Sisterhood is not to be added to the College:

. . . I have promised the patrons, who are a little nervous on that point, that it shall not be so. It will, I hope, eventually be settled in a house, which I have in my eye, and which is very well suited for the purpose in this town. I trust that then we shall always have a sister in the College, taking perhaps its superintendence by turn; and that the proximity of the chapel and its services, may be a comfort to all. At the present moment, however, its first beginning will be at Rotherfield. . . .[1]

This letter shows that Neale at first had considered attaching the Sisterhood to Sackville College, but because of the anxiety of the patrons about this he did not pursue the idea.

The Community started with a few Sisters at Sackville College early in 1855. Miss Ann Gream, daughter of the rector of Rotherfield, some fourteen miles from East Grinstead, took her religious vows in June 1855 and became the first Superior. She still, however, had to look after her father, and for this reason a small house was taken in Rotherfield. It was in this house that the Sisters resided when not engaged in external work.

Miss Gream continued to reside at the rectory (Rotherfield), but constantly visited "St Margaret's", for so she wished it called. She loved this little house dearly. But Mr Neale's constant visits to it were far too great a tax on his time and strength. He made nothing of walking the fourteen miles and back if no conveyance was at hand.[2]

About a year later Neale had a dangerous accident in some conveyance when he was visiting Rotherfield. This nearly cost him his life, and it was soon after decided that the Sisters' home must be moved to East Grinstead.

[1] Unpublished letters at St Margaret's Convent, East Grinstead.
[2] *Memoir*, p. 321b.

A house close to the College was taken, and they moved into it in June 1856. And very wonderfully, the same week that the change was decided on, old Mr Gream was seized with his last illness... and his daughter, then aged forty-seven, came to take charge of the new home.[1]

The following account from the *St Margaret's Magazine* gives some idea of the work and difficulties encountered at Rotherfield. They must have been typical of what the Sisters experienced in many other parts later:

On a lonely spur of Saxonbury Hill, about five miles from Tunbridge Wells and in the parish of Rotherfield, beautifully situated, but abominable in themselves, stood three cottages, in one of which a poor woman was slowly dying of consumption. The place is called Woodside. . . . Hither, then, Mr Neale brought a Sister, July 13th, 1855, and the woman was nursed till the time of her death in March 1856, the Sisters taking it in turn to be with her. The family was large, and there was no sleeping room to be had in the house. A loft was hired in a cottage three or four hundred yards off; the further end was roughly screened off by a sheet hung across, to form a bedroom. . . . The ceiling was nothing but thatch, reaching almost to the floor on both sides. Lonely and cold; wind howling under the eaves, moon and stars shining through holes in the roof, snow drifting in on winter nights, mice holding high games at unseasonable hours, spiders and such other small creatures abundant. "Such extremity of wretchedness", wrote Mr Neale, "I never saw but in Portugal." In that hovel was solved the problem whether Sisters could live with the poor as poor. Sometimes Mrs Bridger's husband was out, and then the Sister slept at the cottage. If he were at home, she returned at night to her loft—greeted as she went into Mrs Knight's cottage, maybe, with, "Come in, Miss; you can have your tea; pig has had his supper." Pig was by far the more important lodger of the two. . . . All kinds of cottage work she had to do: she took care of the baby, mended the clothes, dressed the younger children, cooked, and looked after the house, as well as attending to her patient.

All sorts of difficulties were encountered by the Sisters, and called for much ingenuity to overcome:

There was no proper grate or range, only a couple of stones to make even the household fire on. The Sister . . . had to go into the forest to get wood and then that had to be dried; and when she thought a little stock was provided for the day's use, as likely as not the children burnt it up while she was out of their way. The difficulty of lighting or keeping a fire at all under such circumstances was extreme,

[1] Ibid., p. 322b.

and every expedient was resorted to avoid it. The Sister, for instance, would wrap up an egg in damp paper, and put it in hot ashes to cook. Then the washing, the drawing water. . . . The children took whooping cough, and gave it to the Sister. She had it severely, but remained at her post.[1]

There were many other instances of heroic work on the part of the Sisters.

The Bishop of Chichester (Gilbert), in spite of the fact that he had inhibited Neale, gave his blessing to the Sisterhood in its early days. In a letter to his former tutor, the Reverend William Russell, of Shepperton, dated September 1856, Neale wrote:

But what takes up most of my time is the Sisterhood. They are now settled in a very nice house between us and the Church, close to the College: there are nine of them at present. The Bishop, when confirming here, called on them and gave them his blessing.[2]

From the above we notice that in the second year of the existence of the Sisterhood there were nine Sisters. Such good progress was made that on 30 October 1857 Neale was able to write the following to the Reverend J. S. Haskoll:

The success of the Sisterhood is really surprising. About ten weeks ago, the Archdeacon (Otter), with great fear and trembling, sent for a Sister to nurse a most loathsome cancer case; about a month ago he sent for another Sister, for a malignant typhus; and on Monday last he actually came over—twenty-three—miles to ask that the first Sister might continue to stay, it having been arranged that she was then to leave. Considering the tremendous opposition we have encountered, is not that a triumph over prejudices? We have had scarlet fever again in the House—our latest come Sister has it, and she is now in a precarious state from its tendency to dropsy.[3]

In the same year a small orphanage was taken over by the Sisterhood. This had been started by Neale's sister, Elizabeth, at Brighton. She had had to give up the orphanage, as she was starting a Sisterhood in the parish of St George-in-the-East, Stepney. This Sisterhood became the Community of the Holy Cross. A small house was taken in East Grinstead for the orphanage, and it was named St Katherine's. Two Sisters were placed in charge.[4]

---

[1] Ibid., pp. 318b ff.
[2] Ibid., p. 19d.
[3] Ibid., p. 109d.
[4] A. T. Cameron, *Religious Communities of the Church of England* (1918), p. 71.

Later that year the notorious Lewes riots took place, and the Sisterhood suffered a great setback. Miss Emily Scobell (Sister Amy), the daughter of the Reverend John Scobell of Lewes, had joined the Sisterhood against her father's wishes. Soon afterwards she contracted scarlet fever and died. In her will she left £400 to the Sisterhood. In accordance with her father's wishes it was arranged for the burial to take place at Lewes. In the churchyard after the service Neale and the Sisters were attacked by a mob, and only escaped with great difficulty. Scobell had alleged that his daughter had been inveigled into the Sisterhood by Neale, purposely placed in the way of infection, and influenced on her deathbed to make a will in favour of the Sisterhood. There is little doubt that the riot at the funeral was incited by Scobell. The charges against Neale were of course grossly untrue, and Neale in a special pamphlet refuted them all. But much damage was done to the good name of the Sisterhood. The Bishop of Chichester withdrew from the Community what little support he had given. Some friends fell away, and subscriptions declined. However, various influential laymen took action on behalf of Neale and the Sisterhood, and gradually confidence was restored.[1]

On 21 September 1858 Neale wrote in his diary:

I wonder what will be the result of this Sisterhood. If my life and health and strength are spared, I do believe it may be a great thing. Without extraneous help, without money, with so much opposition, and such episcopal difficulties, it is marvellous that in three years one should have collected ten Sisters, besides the dear one who is with God;—should have the children;—should have such a house; and with the expense of two previous houses; and no anxiety about money. Above all their trust in me

> Doth with a twofold vigour lift me up
> To reach at victory above my head.

I believe that the management of a Sisterhood is my vocation. I see innumerable faults and blunders I have made; but on the whole what a success it has been! Well, for the future, if God will be with me, if he will increase their numbers, and guide and guard us all, I will work harder than I have ever done in His service.[2]

In spite of many difficulties and setbacks, he evidently found much to encourage him in his great undertaking.

---

[1] *Memoir*, pp. 117d f.
[2] Ibid., p. 216d.

We have already seen that Neale in his second novel, *Ayton Priory*, had expressed his ideas about the revival of the Religious Life in the Church of England. This book was written some twelve years before the founding of the Society of St Margaret. In the practical working of a Sisterhood, Neale had to test his theories. Like all the founders of religious communities in the nineteenth century, he had to feel his way. But his profound knowledge of the subject, and his clarity of vision, enabled him to see better than many of his contemporaries the requirements and the possibilities of the Religious Life. We shall now consider briefly Neale's developed ideas on three aspects of this subject: (1) Religious Vows; (2) Types of Religious Orders; (3) The Mass and the Divine Office in a Religious Community.

RELIGIOUS VOWS

When Neale wrote *Ayton Priory*, he saw that religious vows were desirable for the stability of the Religious Life, but he had doubts as to whether they were practicable in the Church of England at that time. From his own experience with the Society of St Margaret he came to see that religious vows were really necessary. A. M. Allchin has shown what a stumbling-block to many the question of vows was in the early days of the revival in the nineteenth century.[1] W. J. Butler (founder of the Wantage Sisters) and T. T. Carter (founder of the Clewer Sisters), under the influence of Bishop Samuel Wilberforce, at first held that irrevocable vows were unscriptural. Later Carter modified his views. But Neale from the beginning, like Pusey, saw the necessity of vows. We shall here quote at some length from a lecture entitled *Sisterhoods of the Church of England*, which was given by Neale in 1865. As this was given in the year before he died, it can be said to give his mature views on the subject of vows:

First let me say that I thank God, with all my heart, that there are many sisterhoods which have no vows at all, neither for a time, nor for life. There are sisterhoods of this kind, both in the English and the Roman Churches. Yet on the whole . . . I believe those sisters are happier as ours of St Margaret's, who are privileged to be able to take vows. I observe several other priests in this room tonight, and would any one of them, I should like to ask, feel happier if he could

[1] A. M. Allchin, *The Silent Rebellion* (1958), pp. 74f.

at any time throw off his clerical character, and become a layman. I am sure the answer of us all would be, "God forbid!" Again how would any woman like, when she came as a bride to her husband, to be married to him for a certain time, say for two or three years, and at the end of that period, if she repented of her choice, to be free?

He then discusses the assertion that Sisters should not be bound to a life they know nothing about:

In the first place, no sister in any English sisterhood can possibly be received as a probationer, or, which is the same thing as a novice without knowing that she is to remain so for two years before she can take the life vow. This being received as a novice stands precisely in the same relation to her future vows as any woman's engagement in this world to her marriage. I wonder how many people are engaged two years before they are married, and how many people have to go through a severe scrutiny as to whether, in the first place, they are fit to be engaged at all, and then after undergoing two years probation as to whether they are fit to be married. . . . I will boldly say there is not one married woman in England, who ought to have the tenth part of the confidence that she will remain steadfast in that state of life to which it has pleased God to call her, that the confirmed sister has. . . . Oh, if you did but know—ay, if you could but see—how the brightest and happiest of all human creatures are sisters thoroughly engaged in their work; if you could but see how these novices come out of their probationary state like caterpillars turned into butterflies, and how they long to take the vow, you would all agree with me as to the absurdity of using the terms "bondage" and "misery" in reference to such a state.

Neale then deals with the scriptural aspect of the subject, which was a bone of contention with many of the opponents of religious vows:

They tell us that all these things are unscriptural. *Dost thou appeal unto Caesar? Unto Caesar thou shalt go.* We clergy know that one chief argument we have against those who say that children ought not to be baptized in their infant days is this—"The Jewish child was brought into covenant with God at eight days old, and if our children are not to have this privilege, so far from being in a better state than the Jews we are in a worse state. If a child amongst us is not to be brought into covenant with God until he or she is fifteen or sixteen years old, whereas the Jewish child enjoyed the privilege when eight days old, there is no comparison between the two systems." This is very true, and we may bring forward a similar argument with reference to women's vows. From Leviticus we find that women were not only allowed to take vows, but that a special privilege was extended to them. If a woman took a vow, and her husband or her father did not say, "No", either at the time or the first moment that they heard the woman had taken it, it stood good, even though the husband or the father might change his mind afterwards. Are Christian women in a lower state than the Jews? We know much better. . . . That makes the end of all I have to say, in which some of us, perhaps, may not quite agree.[1]

The last sentence shows that Neale realized how strong the opposition to vows was, but he was convinced that they were necessary and right. To-day it is taken for granted that lifelong vows are necessary for the stability of the Religious Life.

TYPES OF RELIGIOUS ORDERS

It is quite clear that Neale intended the Society of St Margaret to be a religious order engaged in active work in the world, with prayer, of course, as the basis of all its work. In a sermon to the Sisters he explains the different types of religious orders as follows:

You know very well the two great divisions into which our dear Lord's servants are cast—the secular and the Religious life. So in the Religious life, there are different stages, from those who only give themselves to prayer, to those whose chief end and aim is work. See how it is abroad. The Carmelites were an entirely ascetic order. They had fallen off in their zeal. They were neither one thing, nor yet another. They were cloistered, therefore they could not act as Sisters of Charity. They were corrupt, therefore they could not act as Sisters who lived for prayer. It pleased God to raise up St Theresa. A certain portion, perhaps the third, of the order followed her reform, that is, returned to the original rules of the Carmelites. These are the most cloistered order. They neither teach nor visit, nor help sinners in any outward way. They only pray; and by their prayers doubtless they win great battles, and they lead what is in and by itself the higher life.

Then at the very other end of the scale, come the Beguines, who are entirely given to the work of Sisters of Mercy; who do not even take vows of perpetual chastity; and who have little, very little time for prayer. . . .

And so of you, my Sisters: of all the Sisterhoods in the English Church you have the duty which gives you hardest work and least prayer. . . .

It has pleased God to give to me *you*, a Sisterhood banded together for work; sometimes for *terrible* work, in the first place; for prayer in the second. Your motto is: He that works well prays well. Others

[1] *Sisterhoods of the Church of England,* a lecture delivered by the Rev. J. M. Neale, D.D. (1865).

have to do with those who have prayer in the first place; work in the second. Their motto is: He that prays well works well. Both most true.[1]

These words show that Neale intended his Sisterhood to be engaged in active work in the world. The rule provides for the recital of the whole of the Divine Office (including the night office), besides the daily Mass, and one and a half hours of private prayer. Thus the rule of the Society is an expression of what is known as the mixed life, which combines both contemplation and active work in the world. It is as such that the rule is interpreted to-day. The active work consists of works of mercy, spiritual and corporal, especially among the sick, the poor, and orphans.

In another place Neale describes the different kinds of active Sisterhoods as follows:

For you know that, however much in common conversation you are called Sisters of Mercy, your proper title is Sisters of Charity. Sisters of Mercy are they who visit the sick . . . Sisters of Compassion are those who teach the young . . . Sisters of Fidelity are they who receive penitents . . . but Sisters of Charity have all these, and many other occupations. . . .[2]

The rule of the Society of St Margaret is described as follows:

If it be asked on what Rule that of St Margaret was grounded, the answer certainly is, on that of the Visitation, as it was originally designed by St Francis de Sales, before he was over-persuaded to make it a cloistered order, and so, as has been said, left St Vincent de Paul to pick up the crown which his Sisters had laid down. Parts of the internal Rule are identical, and the spirit of the "Entretiens Spirituels" was exactly that which inspired the instructions given to St Margaret's Sisters. For this was to be essentially a Missionary Sisterhood, living in an atmosphere of fresh air, and mingling very largely with the world outside: the Sisters making themselves all things to all men, if by any means they might save some: going forth open-handed and open-hearted to face all manner of unlooked for emergencies, and on occasions to forego all means of grace; and yet to hold them fast by God, to endure as seeing Him who is invisible, to anchor all their faith and hope and love in their dear Lord, serving Him and suffering for Him in His suffering creatures, and drawn away from His love and service by no temptations, whether on the right hand or on the left. It was a tremendous undertaking, and so it was felt to be both by the Sisters and their Founder.[3]

[1] Neale, *Sermons for Feast Days*, pp. 78–81.
[2] *Sermons for the Church Year*, New Edition 1897, vol. i, pp. 218f—preached 1859.
[3] *Memoir*, p. 10d.

THE MASS AND THE DIVINE OFFICE

From the beginning Neale saw that the community life must centre round and derive its spiritual strength from the Eucharist and the Divine Office. In the Constitutions of the Society it is stated that "as Jesus represented by His poor is to be the object of their active work", so he "yet more lowly as present in the Blessed Sacrament, shall be the central light of their devotion". Their work is to be offered "to His glory in that Blessed Sacrament, and in reparation for the dishonour He endures that He may be among His creatures". Because of this devotion to our Lord in the Blessed Sacrament a daily Mass was highly desirable, if not a necessity. The daily Mass was started in St Margaret's Oratory, the Sisters' chapel, on 13 July 1856.[1] A year later they had perpetual reservation of the Blessed Sacrament, and Benediction was introduced in 1859. It is remarkable how quickly Neale arrived at this position. He was almost certainly the first priest in the nineteenth century to revive the practice of perpetual reservation in the Church of England. To-day every Anglican religious community takes a daily Mass and reservation for granted, but this was by no means the case in the early days of the revival. It was not until 1887 (twenty-one years after Neale's departure from this life) that the Eucharist came to be offered daily in the chapel of the Community of St Mary the Virgin at Wantage. In the same Community the first Midnight Mass at Christmas was not celebrated until 1898, whereas Neale had this in 1855.[2]

All who were concerned with the revival of the Religious Life in England in the nineteenth century realized that the Divine Office, as expressed in the Book of Common Prayer, would need to be supplemented with the traditional hours of prayer. In *Ayton Priory* Neale had suggested that the Bishops might sanction the use of a form of Compline to use with Matins and Evensong. But from experience Neale came to see that, whereas the Book of Common Prayer Matins and Evensong were very convenient for secular priests, they were not adequate for a religious community. And so we find that in the Society of St Margaret the traditional hours of prayer did not simply supplement the Divine

[1] J. M. Neale, *Sermons on the Blessed Sacrament* (1870), p. 11.
[2] Peter F. Anson, *The Call of the Cloister* (1955), p. 249.

Office in the Prayer Book, but supplanted it. In the rule provision is made for Prayer Book Matins and Evensong on Sundays, but not on weekdays. Here Neale differed from Butler and Carter, who kept the Prayer Book offices and supplemented them with the traditional lesser hours. The Society of St Margaret was also the first to use an English translation of the Night Office.[1]

From all this it is clear that Neale had a firmer grasp of the essentials of the Religious Life than many of his contemporaries. His profound knowledge and clarity of vision enabled him to see better than others the essential elements for the establishment and stability of a religious community.

There are two events which offer some testimony to the capability of Neale as a restorer of the Religious Life in the Church of England. The first event concerns the Eastern Church, in which of course he had a great interest. After the Crimean War the Russian Church sent two ladies to East Grinstead to obtain information about nursing religious Sisters in England. At that time there were apparently no active religious Sisters in Russia.

Anxious to learn how the system [of nursing sisters] worked in England, the Russian Church sent two ladies to gather information at East Grinstead; and acting upon their report and upon the knowledge gained during their residence with the St Margaret's Sisters, determined to establish Sisterhoods upon the same lines. It was a circumstance that, in the midst of many discouragements, greatly gladdened their Founder's heart; one of the things for which he said he thanked God most, that, in some measure, he had been able to benefit the Communion he so deeply venerated.[2]

It is surely a remarkable tribute to Neale that members of the Russian Church should seek his guidance in this matter.

The second event was the opening of an independent daughter house in Aberdeen in 1864. Neale refers to this in a sermon as the first since the Reformation:

We cannot all of us but thank God and take courage too, that now, for the first time since the Reformation, that here, and that among us, a Religious House has had the vitality to send off an independent child, to be closely united, let us hope for ever, with herself, but owing no obedience to her.[3]

[1] Allchin, op. cit., p. 108.
[2] Towle, *Memoir*, p. 278.
[3] Neale, *Sermons on Passages of the Psalms* (1871), p. 149.

This expansion of the Society, for which Neale had prayed from the beginning, is a further testimony to the importance of his work for the restoration of the Religious Life. The subsequent growth of the Society, and its strength to-day, are in no small measure due to the firm foundations laid by him and his grasp of the essential principles of the monastic life.

The Society of St Margaret, in spite of opposition and setbacks, grew steadily. In 1861 there were fifteen Sisters, presumably all professed.[1] At the time of Neale's death (1866) there were about forty professed Sisters. In 1867 the Reverend J. S. Haskoll, Neale's friend and literary executor wrote:

> What a joy to remember the *three* Sisters at St Margaret's ten years before, and then to think of the *more than forty* who in his last illness were gathered under its different roofs! Not that he ever attributed in any way this success to his own efforts, except as an instrument in God's hands. "A Domino factum est istud, et est mirabile in oculis nostris." These words were for ever on his lips.[2]

We shall conclude this survey of Neale's work as a restorer of the Religious Life in the Church of England, by trying to convey some idea of the spirit of the Society to which he gave so much. We have seen that the rule of the Society is that of the mixed life of prayer and work. The Society has a special devotion to the Name of Jesus, by which our Lord willed himself to be known in his Incarnation. An insight into its spirit is given in a letter written by Mother Kate. Kate Egerton-Warburton had joined the Society at the age of eighteen in 1858, and so was one of the early members. She later became the Mother Superior of the daughter house of St Saviour's Priory, Haggerston, where she did magnificent work. It has been said that her devotion during the smallpox epidemics in that part of London is "a golden page in Anglican history."[3] She died in 1923 at the age of eighty-three. In the latter years of her life she wrote of her early days at East Grinstead:

> I have always felt thankful that my lot was cast in the Community of St Margaret. There was a sort of breadth and large-mindedness about its foundation,—a sort of what we nowadays call Christian Socialism about it, which has always appealed to me intensely, and makes one feel one is not a round peg in a square hole, but a bullet

[1] *Letters*, p. 337.
[2] Neale, *Sermons on the Song of Songs* (1867), pp. vi f.
[3] Desmond Morse-Boycott, *They Shine Like Stars* (1947), p. 128.

fitting into a billet. Apart from his intellectual and literary gifts, Dr Neale's sympathy and interest fascinated me, and not the least of his attractive qualities was his love of suffering humanity and of animals. It has been a joy through all one's Mission work in London, to recall the happy old days of early St Margaret's: the peaceful little Oratory, where all the Founder's sermons on the Religious Life were preached, where his wonderful Bible classes on the mystical interpretation of Holy Scripture and his interesting instructions to the children were given; where we knelt, not in choir, but each at her own little Prie-Dieu, which, as he so often reminded us, was to every one a little Sanctuary set apart for each soul's devotions and communings with God. I can recall it all so vividly, the narrow dark little Oratory, with three plain wooden arches shutting in the Sanctuary, where the red lamp flickered in the semi-darkness, and the tall figure of the Founder stood before the altar, speaking words of comfort, encouragement and, where he deemed it necessary, of the very sharpest reproof. If we did not, all and each of us, join heartily in the singing, if we did not make all the responses together clearly and audibly, if strict adherence to the rule had seemed to slacken, if through any carelessness on the Sister's part things had not gone quite straight at the orphanage,—all these were spoken about quite plainly in stern reproof for doing the Master's work half-heartedly.

The associations of those early St Margaret's days are such a vision of peace, brimful of aspirations, hopes and longings, which have now either died away or ripened into maturity, a maturity how very short of the aspirations! There was always such a homey, happy earnestness about the early St Margaret's, so full, as I said of aspiration. Nothing seemed too great to attempt, nothing seemed too high or too remote to hope for. We would, I believe, have dared or done anything. It was wonderful how the influence of such a marvellously brave, enthusiastic spirit as our Founder's permeated every one of us. We always had the example of the Saints and Martyrs put before us: the Gates of Gold and the City of the Lamb were always glittering before our eyes. Pain, shame and suffering seemed as nothing for the glory, which should be revealed to those who bore all for His sake. . . . There was a consciousness of God's Saints actually round and about us, which moved and inspired us to do and to dare anything and everything. The greater part of those whom he trained personally have passed away to their Eternal Rest, but we few stragglers who are left look back as a traveller might from the summit of a rough road into the golden glow, which veils the far away horizon. . . .[1]

An interesting insight into Neale's concern for details is his choice of colour for the Sisters' habit. As their work was to be

[1] Unpublished letter of Mother Kate at St Saviour's Priory, Haggerston, London, E.

partly among children, he rejected black, which he considered gloomy, and chose grey. Tradition says that he arrived at this colour by mixing all the liturgical colours on a palette. The result was a dark grey.

He did not wish his Sisters to be morose and dull. He wanted them to be happy and joyful. In a sermon to them he said:

> God forbid that you should ever put on a sort of behaviour or appearance that you think Sisters ought to have. It is the most dear thing to me, when I can hear, as I did the other day, of a Sister: "she was the life of the children's party"; and you know not the help it was to those who were doubting about such a service of God.[1]

The gaiety of the East Grinstead Sisters is referred to in the obituary notice to Neale in *The Guardian*, 15 August 1866. After referring to the severity of the rule it says of the Sisters:

> Their gaiety is due to the eminently glad and hopeful form in which religion was set before them by their Director, who freely lavished on their instruction the marvellous stores of his learning. Instead of committing the grave error of feminising his sermons and counsels because he had only women to deal with, he aimed at showing them the masculine side of Christianity also, to teach them its strength as well as its beauty.[2]

Neale was never daunted by any task or any opposition however formidable it might be. If he knew a particular piece of work was right and in accordance with the will of God, he went forward with it, regardless of the cost and suffering to himself. One of his favourite sayings was: "If it is possible, it *shall* be done; and if it is impossible, it *must* be done." Through his faith, devotion, and persistence the Society of St Margaret was launched on its way, and the growth and strength of the Society is in no small measure due to the firm foundations which the Founder laid. He accomplished with his Sisters that which Roman Sisters had said was impossible outside their own Communion. Indeed the Abbess of a Hungarian convent is quoted as saying to him: "I could not have believed that grace to do such works could have been found in members of the English Church."[3]

We conclude with a further quotation from Mother Kate, who owed much to Dr Neale, and who in her life as a religious

---

[1] Neale, *Sermons on the Apocalypse etc.* (New Edition, 1897), p. 205.
[2] Quoted by A. M. Allchin, *The Silent Rebellion* (1958), p. 99.
[3] A leaflet, *John Mason Neale*, R. S. H., 1866(?), at St Margaret's Convent.

showed so much of the spirit which he tried to foster in the Society of St Margaret:

> Like all other men who have accomplished great things he was most careful in details, and this, not only with regard to the inner religious life of the Sisters, but with everything appertaining to the outward part. If he met the orphans going for a walk, and one child had on an odd pinafore . . . the orphanage Sister received a severe reprimand. When he brought a friend to look over the orphanage, and found stray articles from a previous sewing class, left scattered about, he made no remark at the time, but severely censured the Sister in charge of the room afterwards, saying, "If you are not careful in small matters, how will it be when you have larger work entrusted to you?"

> He was most particular in the recital of the Office, that every Sister should make the responses clearly and distinctly, and not mumble them in her throat. As far as I can remember no detail passed unnoticed by him, and this was the man who could with a few burning words take you straight up from earth to Paradise, into the company of the Blessed Saints! No man so combined earth and heaven. He was in a peculiar way linked with the other world, as he had that power, given to so few, of having glimpses of the supernatural. . . .

> With his intense love of nature and appreciation of all its beauties, it was a joy to him that the greater part of his life was lived in one of the most picturesque parts of lovely Sussex, and it is there stands his memorial, in the red-roofed, many gabled Convent of St Margaret's. From there have gone his daughters bearing their lamps to America, Africa, and India,[1] each endeavouring in God's name, to be a burning and a shining light to help those souls among whom she has been sent to work. These had all his earnest prayers while he was yet on earth, and we know they have all, wherever their lot be cast, his still more earnest prayers in Paradise.[2]

[1] Mother Kate meant Ceylon: the Sisters have not worked in India.
[2] *St Margaret's Half-Yearly Chronicle* (1918), vol. v, part 1, 1 Jan.

7

The Need for Good English Hymns

NEALE'S time at East Grinstead was by no means wholly devoted to Sackville College and the founding of the Society of St Margaret. In spite of all the energy he put into these works he found time for an extraordinary amount of literary work, which was to make its mark on the whole Church. In the introduction to the Sackville College Sermons we are given a delightful picture of his study adjoining the chapel in Sackville College:

> Drawing aside a curtain in the ante-chapel . . . we find ourselves in the Warden's study. And what a study! An absolute honeycomb of bookshelves. Lined with books, hung across with books, books in the middle, books everywhere: except in the space occupied by the carved oak mantelpiece, which is jewelled with a lovely collection of icons; and a narrow passage allowing just sufficient room to move amongst the pervading bookshelves. Hither come scholars, and the letters of scholars, from far and near, Oxford and Cambridge, London and Dublin, Russia and America, propounding knotty points for elucidation in theology, politics, hymnology, liturgiology, canon law and history. And the Warden, master of some twenty languages, and of an immense mass of varied learning, the first liturgical scholar of his day, and endowed with foresight amounting (as subsequent events have proved) almost to prophecy, writes there behind his desk, shy, retiring, assuming nothing but his own inadequacy to instruct, and yet ready with a satisfactory answer to almost every question. Besides replies to these individual applications, his unresting pen pours forth work upon work, with marvellous rapidity, learning, and versatility.[1]

Though hymns were only a part of Neale's literary work, it is as a hymn writer that he is generally known to-day by the majority of people. His interest in hymns went back to his childhood. He was brought up in a very strict evangelical home, and had to

[1] *Sermons Preached in Sackville College Chapel*, vol. i, pp. viii ff.

learn the hymns of Isaac Watts by heart. He found many of them a great trial. One of them started:

> My thoughts on awful subjects roll,
> Damnation and the dead.

Of this his daughter wrote:

A family treasure of his (Watts') "Psalms and Hymns" containing this terrible one and many such, is in my possession. . . . The family, therefore, were brought up under Dr Watts' and kindred teaching, and it was to free children from this "yoke", as he calls it, that John Mason Neale wrote his first hymns.[1]

In a letter to Benjamin Webb, dated All Souls' Day 1842, Neale wrote about his *Hymns for Children,* which was published in 1843:

Long ago I determined that if no one else did anything to free our poor children from the yoke of Watts, I would try. I have been seriously at work at it the last six weeks, and have accomplished a little volume of 34.[2]

At the same time that he was working on hymns for children, he was also working on a collection of hymns for the sick. His own illness, which caused him to go to Madeira in 1843, was no doubt partly the origin of this collection. After this there was hardly any period of his life when he was not concerned with hymns.

In this work, as with most of his undertakings, Neale had to plough new furrows and to meet with strong opposition. Not all the followers of the Catholic revival approved of the introduction of hymns into the worship of the Church of England. Webb attributed Neale's concern about hymns to "the slough of evangelicalism which clung to him".[3] In an article on hymns towards the end of his life Neale refers to the fact that the early Tractarians, "sickened with the vulgarity and heresy of many of the then popular hymns, set their faces against all hymnology, and would have either Tate and Brady, or Sternhold and Hopkins, and nothing else".[4]

Following this line himself, Webb wrote to Neale on 1 September 1849 as follows:

---

[1] *Letters*, p. 45.
[2] Ibid., p. 46.
[3] Towle, *Memoir*, p. 208.
[4] *The Christian Remembrancer*, vol. xlvi (July 1863), p. 106.

I expect I shall loathe your Methodistical snuffling hymnizing article. It is the oddest thing to me that you have never slipped off that Evangelical slough: and is due, I take it, to your own fatal facility of versifying.[1]

Neale's "facility of versifying" is shown by the fact that he won the Seatonian Prize Poem eleven years in succession, starting in 1845.[2] But Neale strongly refuted his friend's accusations in the following letter, which gives a good account of his ideas on the subject of vernacular hymns at this time:

As we are in the controversial line, we will now proceed to Hymns. ... Now, I wish you would seriously think whether you are not prejudiced on the subject, whether you are not guilty of high-and-dryism. You can only say your hatred of hymns means one of three things:

(a) That there should be no hymns in the Offices of the Church Catholic.

(b) That there *should* be no vernacular hymns in our language.

(c) That there *are* no vernacular hymns in our own English.

I will not believe that you mean the first; I agree with you in the third, with very few exceptions. Now as to the second.

This comes the worse from you, because you used to be in favour of a vernacular Liturgy and Offices, or Offices, at least. Now, for my part, I am not; *but*, while we have prayers in English, why are we not to have hymns? Did ever any Church, or any body of religious whatever, do without them? Surely the language that can bear to be used in the prayers, can be sufficient for the hymns of the Church. Now, in my article, which is a long one, I have taken a great deal of pains to set forth what I am sure—and what I have been sure of ever since I thought at all on the subject—are the kind of practical suggestions we want. I was six months writing the article, and six years at least thinking of it; therefore I shall be very sorry if you "loathe" it. The principle of it is, that a Hymnologion must be had; that it cannot be made to order; that the Church has a perfect right to select and adapt the compositions of heretics in this, as in everything else, to her own use; that, notwithstanding, in the original hymn-books (which I go through) there are not above ten or twelve hymns that would do; that there are ten or twelve; that the translations from the Breviary are generally speaking, wretched; that to the Breviary, however, we must go, taking care not to select trashy hymns from it; that with revision we may get twenty or thirty fair translations. Then I make some remarks on the usual fault of translations from the Breviary: that there will thus be thirty or forty hymns provided, as a tentative Hymnology, with which at present we must be content. Now I confess that for my part I see no

[1] *Letters*, p. 124.   [2] Towle, *Memoir*, p. 129.

approach to cant in this. You pooh-pooh hymns as Paley pooh-poohed Regeneration, because the word and thing had been abused. As to what you say about my not having cast the slough of Evangelicalism, I don't think it is true, at least in the sense you mean. Subjectively it may be. And as for my standing up for hymns, because I—or any fool—can write rhymes, that is too absurd. No; you profess not to like any poetry; therefore, of course, not hymns. I am more liberal; I don't enter into painting, but I don't pooh-pooh pictures in Churches.[1]

Webb evidently remained quite unconvinced at the time, for in his reply to Neale he writes:

But I don't believe that we can have hymns in the vernacular. I don't believe that we subjective men can write hymns, which must be altogether objective. You and others may make uncommonly pretty imitations: but they are only like leaves of the Rejected Addresses. The ancient hymns are bald, meagre, rude, etc., etc., but with all this there is in them a simplicity, a vigour, a freshness, a heart, that one loves them. Homer could write a cookery scene, and make his heroes eat guts, and we love to read it: and you might imitate just such another, but how should we esteem it? I, too, have thought many years on this subject, and am more and more convinced that the *age* of hymns has passed. Happy those who can use the ancient Latin ones: with our vernacular we have lost our privilege. It is the same thing throughout: the translation into English reduced everything to common sense—the curse or the glory (as you choose) of our present ritual. I am not convinced either, on *a priori* grounds, about the *possibility* of English hymns. The necessity of rhyme as well as metre, and the difficulties of English rhyme must not be overlooked. . . . What doggerel and balderdash are our two versions! intolerable, even though redeemed (as still more modern compositions cannot be) by a certain quaintness and difference from familiar forms of speech. I doubt, in short, the possibility of the language of common life, in such an age as this, being fit for this sort of composition. . . .[2]

We have quoted this letter at length, because it shows how vehement was Webb's attack on the idea of vernacular hymns. Neale's reply to this letter unfortunately is not preserved, but he evidently had a good answer to Webb's arguments, because it was not long before Webb was converted to his views in the matter. Less than a year later, on 2 August 1850, we find Neale writing to his friend as follows:

I quite agree with you about the desirableness of having the Gregorian Hymns well sung before all are printed off. But it will be

[1] *Letters*, pp. 124f.   [2] Ibid., pp. 126f.

much more useful for correcting what is written than for the first translation. When I have a dozen or so ready I should like to come over to you and try the Latin and the English. . . .[1]

It is clear from this that Webb was persuaded to help Neale in the production of a collection of hymns translated from the Latin, which was sponsored by the Ecclesiological Society. The title of this collection was *Hymnal Noted*. Part I was published in 1851. We shall consider it more in detail in a later chapter. Suffice it to say now that Webb became one of the editors with Neale, and he translated himself one of the hymns, *O Amor Quam Extaticus,* which appeared in Part II, published in 1856. This hymn subsequently appeared in all editions of *Hymns Ancient and Modern*,[2] and also in *The English Hymnal*.

Thus Neale won over Webb, and with him no doubt many others, to the necessity of vernacular hymns. It seems incredible to-day that there should have been this kind of opposition to hymns. We cannot imagine the Church of England without hymns now, and we may be thankful to Neale, not only for giving to the Church so many good hymns in the vernacular, both translations and original compositions, but also for converting those of the Catholic party who at first opposed the use of vernacular hymns in the services of the Church.

The article on hymns to which reference has been made above appeared in *The Christian Remembrancer* in 1849. It is a comprehensive survey of English hymns up to that date, and shows what Neale thought of the various collections of hymns which had already been made. At the head of the article there is a list of no less than twenty-six collections of hymns, starting with those of Isaac Watts. Neale surveys them all, and the article concludes with recommendations and suggestions for future translations and selections of hymns. In the letter to Webb, quoted above, Neale says that he had been six months writing this article, and at least six years thinking about it. As he was a rapid thinker and writer, we are given some idea of how thoroughly he had studied this subject.

The article begins by deploring the loss of hymns in the Church

[1] Ibid., p. 154.
[2] *Hymns Ancient and Modern* (Historical Edition, 1909), p. 829 (Hymn 173 in the Standard Edition).

through the introduction of the vernacular into the services at the Reformation:

> Those noble hymns, which had solaced anchorets on their mountains, monks in their cells, priests in bearing up against the burden and heat of the day, missionaries in girding themselves for martyrdom—henceforth they became as a sealed book and a dead letter. The prayers and collects, the versicles and responses, of the earlier Church might, without any great loss of beauty, be preserved; but the hymns, whether of the sevenfold daily office, of the weekly commemoration of creation and redemption, of the yearly revolution of the Church's seasons, or of the birthdays to the glory of martyrs and confessors—those hymns by which day unto day had uttered speech, and night unto night had taught knowledge—they could not, by the hands then employed in ecclesiastical matters, be rendered into another, and that a then comparatively barbarous tongue. One attempt the Reformers made—the version of the *Veni Creator Spiritus* in the Ordinal; and that, so far perhaps fortunately, was the only one. Cranmer, indeed, expressed some casual hope that men fit for the office might be induced to come forward; but the very idea of a hymnology of the time of Henry VIII may make us feel thankful that the primate's wish was not carried out.[1]

The Church of England had to wait for the coming of English hymnody. In the meantime she had the Psalms.

> But the people, reduced in great measure to the prose of a read service, clamoured for metrical compositions of some kind, which would necessitate a portion of music; and Sternhold and Hopkins arose to supply the want. With their versions, or rather perversions, of the Psalms, of the Ten Commandments, of the Creed, of the *Te Deum*, and of the other prose hymns of the Church, she was contented for nearly a century and a half. . . .[2]

Between the accession of Elizabeth and Cromwell sacred lyrics were added to our literature by Crashaw, Herbert, Wither, Henry Vaughan, and others, but of these only four were suitable as hymns in Church. After Sternhold and Hopkins came Tate and Brady—"a still lower abyss of wretchedness".[3]

Reference is then made to various hymn-writers of the eighteenth century—Watts, the Wesleys, Doddridge, Cowper, Toplady, and others. As we have seen in connection with children's hymns, Neale had little use for the hymns of Watts (1674–1748). Their theology was heretical, e.g. the denial of the part

---

[1] *The Christian Remembrancer*, vol. xviii (July to Dec. 1849), p. 303.
[2] Ibid., p. 304.
[3] Ibid., p. 306.

which the First Person of the Blessed Trinity bore in the work of man's redemption, and the idea that our Lord's death reconciled God to man, whereas St Paul teaches that it reconciled man to God. Also some of the words of his hymns are "as revolting as profane", e.g. a Eucharistic hymn

> Here every bowel of our God
> With soft compassion rolls.[1]

Neale however recognizes that Watts "has left some few— some very few—pieces, which, with alterations, would grace a hymnology of the English Church". Amongst them he places "When I survey the wondrous Cross", and he even goes to the extent of making a Latin version of it, in order to show its resemblance to hymns of old time.

Of Doddridge (1702–51) he writes:

He evidently took Watts for his model; and while he never equalled that writer in his few really good compositions, he never fell to his vulgarities and profanities.

With reference to the Methodist Hymn Book Neale writes:

One remarkable circumstance connected with these hymns is the popularity they have acquired with the new sceptical school. . . . One reason of this preference is, no doubt, the intense subjectivity of these compositions. . . . Among the Wesleyans it is well known that the Hymn-book has almost usurped the place of the Bible; and translations from it, in the foreign missions, form about the first productions of the Missionary press.

He criticizes "the offensive vulgarity of some of the Wesleyan anapaestic compositions".[2]

As to the theology of these compositions, it is what might be expected. The mischievous Wesleyan idea of the necessity of faith only, for the forgiveness of sins,—in plain words, believe that you are pardoned, and you are pardoned,—is kept, perhaps, more in the background than one might have supposed likely; but the other—and comparatively, innoxious—dogma, of the sinless state of perfection attainable by every Christian, is again and again repeated. Yet, against the worst errors of Calvinism, Wesley takes an opportunity of protesting constantly, and occasionally alters an obnoxious verse, where he admits the hymn of another author.[3]

Neale continues however:

---

[1] Ibid., p. 311.   [2] Ibid., p. 315.   [3] Ibid., p. 316.

It was the boast of Wesley in the Preface . . . "Here are no cant expressions, no words without meaning; those who impute this to us, know not what they say." Yet we will venture to assert, that no hymn book, except the Moravian, contains half so much. This alone, were there no other objections, would ruin some of those attempts which might otherwise be passable.[1]

When he comes to Whitefield (1714–70), Neale says that he had no pretensions to be a writer of verse, and his book contains "specimens of profane vulgarity". But he commends "Sweet the moments rich in blessing" in this collection. He also commends Cennick's "Children of the heavenly King", suggesting some alterations.[2]

Of Toplady (1740–78) Neale says that his is "the only name among English writers who seems fitted to have added greatly to the value of our hymns, had he been brought up in a more perfect knowledge of the truth. . . . 'Rock of Ages cleft for me', is undoubtedly the best original hymn in the English language, provided it be taken as a penitential devotion, and not as the ordinary and proper expression of a Christian's everyday prayers."[3]

Neale's judgement of Newton (1725–1807) is very severe:

Probably, the worst original collection of hymns ever put forth is the Olney Book. In some of Cowper's there may be beauty: but Newton's are the very essence of doggerel. The prosaic structure of his verse is such that we wonder how any rhymester could write them. . . . We may safely affirm that Newton is quite out of the question for Church purposes; or indeed for any Hymn-book whatever, and in whatever sect.[4]

Neale could be very scathing in some of his criticisms, especially with regard to hymns. His judgement of Newton has not been endorsed by later compilers of hymns, most of whom have found a place for some of his hymns.

Of Cowper (1731–1800) Neale writes:

The genius of Cowper, though it certainly never shone less than his hymns, raises them far above his friend's. "There is a fountain filled with blood", might perhaps be admitted as a Lent hymn; while "God moves in a mysterious way", and "God of my life, to Thee I call", we might, without much hesitation, make our own.[5]

[1] Ibid., p. 317. [4] Ibid., p. 319.
[2] Ibid., pp. 318f. [5] Ibid.
[3] Ibid.

The popularity of the Olney book is attributed to the immense influence of Newton.

Neale next considers Bishop Heber (1785–1826), who

deeply deplored the miserable estate of English hymnology, and set himself in earnest to raise it. But how? It was but in a slight degree that he turned to the old sources of Christian devotion; his chief conception was original compositions. He brought an elegant mind, but little else, to the task; and accordingly some elegant verses were the result; some also, we are bound to add, remarkably inelegant.[1]

Reference is then made to other collections of hymns from the Evangelical party:

Pre-eminent among the rest stood the "Percy" collection, the "Simeon" collection, the "Cottage Hymn-book", and Mr Hall's, usually called the Bishop of London's collection, because unhappily dedicated to him: this is one of the worst; and other collections were, generally speaking, nothing but compilations from these. More or less of heresy attached to all of them: happy he that, in a church where a collection was used, got off with irreverence or nonsense.[2]

After this Neale turns to the question of the revival of the ancient hymns of the Church:

The principal sources from which an English reader would derive a knowledge of the Hymns of the Latin Church are the translations, chiefly from the *Roman* Breviary, of Mr Copeland, Bishop Mant, J. Williams (an American author), Mr Newman (in a privately printed translation of the PARS HYMNALIS of the Roman Breviary) and Mr Caswall—who alone has translated *all* the Hymns of the Roman Breviary and Missal; besides those which occur in Anglo-Roman Missals, and in different collections, such as those of Mr Palmer, of Magdalene, and the selection for the use of Margaret-street chapel; while of translations from the Paris Breviary, we have Mr Williams's, Mr Chandler's and the Leeds Hymn-book: the third little more than a transcript however of the second.[3]

According to Neale all these collections fell short of what was wanted. One objection was that a number of the hymns were translations from the Paris and not the Roman Breviary, which was more primitive. Another objection was the extraordinary measures in which the translations were made:

[1] Ibid., p. 320.   [2] Ibid., p. 321.   [3] Ibid., p. 322.

It is the peculiar beauty, indeed, of English, as compared with Latin, that any kind of strophe is allowable; but then it behoves English writers to be more careful, lest this liberty of theirs become licence. Especially is this necessary in translating verse, so simple, so unchanging, as are the greater part of the hymns of the Church. But the translators have often offended in this particular. What a monstrous stanza, for instance, is this:

> Lo! the Baptist's herald cry
> Shakes the Jordan;
> Let the waken'd eye and ear
> Welcome the great Harbinger.[1]

Neale recommends that translations from the Latin should "adopt the same species of verse". This alone can convey a true idea of the original, and it means that the same ancient tune can be used. He then gives some examples of bad translations and concludes:

We have now touched on some of the causes why translations from the Breviary have generally been unsuccessful. But the chief remains —the great carelessness, haste, and slovenliness with which they have been written. This remark applies to every translator, except Mr Wackerbarth. Mr Caswall, too, is less obnoxious to it than the rest.[2]

He then makes the following recommendations about translations:

Let all the versions from the Breviary be collected: let some scholar, possessed of a good ear, and well read in our poets, select the best parts of each, and, where they all fail, endeavour to supply the deficiency with something of his own. Let him be content with thirty or forty good translations; and let him spare no pains in rendering them the model versions: to these let twelve or fifteen best English hymns we at present possess be added;—with such corrections as the Faith may require or taste suggest. Then let the book be submitted to the correction of such members of the English Church as have a right to be consulted; and then let a second editor decide between their corrections, and the original of the first compiler. The forty hymns we so obtain might perhaps be sufficient till some future convocation shall authoritatively decide the great question of Hymnology.[3]

According to Neale the only general attempt to provide a hymn book for the English Church—*Translations from the Roman etc. Breviaries* by Bishop Mant, Copeland, Chandler, Isaac Williams,

---

[1] Ibid., p. 323.   [2] Ibid., p. 329.   [3] Ibid.

J. Williams, Caswall, Wackerbarth, etc., which appeared in 1847—
was an utter failure:

> It contains 236 hymns, evidently raked together with the utmost
> speed, and reminding one of the Wise Man's declaration—"An
> inheritance may be gotten hastily at the beginning: but the end
> thereof shall not be blessed".[1]

The question is then raised as to how far the Church is justified
in selecting for her use the compositions of those who were
never within her fold, some of whom "were tainted with the most
gross and glaring heresy".

> To us, we confess, the question seems perfectly easy. In the same
> way as the Church has dared to inherit the earth physically, and
> intellectually, and aesthetically, so she may vindicate to herself its
> moral possession. It would be as reasonable to say that she should
> not reconcile the temples of heretics,—that she should not avail
> herself of the treasures of Pagans,—that she should not render
> subservient to her own purpose the art or the discoveries of Greece
> or Rome,—that she should not have stamped the Aristotelian
> philosophy with her own approval, and made it that of the school-
> men; as that she may not lay hands, whenever and wherever they
> may occur, on the writings of those that acknowledge her not,
> adopting them either wholly, or moulding them to her own creeds.
> A precisely similar case occurs in the fact that a part of the authentic
> version of the Scriptures, as employed by the Eastern Church is
> actually the work of a heretic.[2] If it be urged that this appropriation
> can only be made by a Synodal Act of a Provincial Church, so far
> we agree: but the Hymnology, the composition of which we are
> contemplating, can only be viewed in the light of a tentative work,
> and subject, of course, to the final approval or rejection of her supreme
> authority. All we urge is, that the hymns of Dissenters will be
> accepted or rejected by Convocation on their own merit or demerit.
> ... And we cannot help expressing our thankfulness that our Church
> has hitherto been kept from committing herself, as her American
> daughter has done, to a hastily compiled and trashy hymn-book. A
> judgement of extreme charity only can hinder us from branding
> some of the compositions of the latter as undoubtedly heretical.[3]

Finally Neale deals with the question of children's hymns,
about which, as we have seen, he had some very strong
convictions:

---

[1] Ibid., p. 334.
[2] Neale was possibly thinking here of Origen and his critical version of the Old
Testament, known as the Hexapla.
[3] Art. cit., pp. 334f.

We now, finally, have to speak of a class of hymns, which completely belongs to modern times: we mean those for children. Till the late movement there were but two original works of this kind which attained any celebrity: Dr Watts' Divine and Moral Songs, and Jane Taylor's Nursery Rhymes. . . . Has any one composition had more influence in forming the minds of English children,—we do not for one moment except the Catechism,—than Watts' Divine and Moral Songs? Is it not a fact, that where the parish priest himself has preached the doctrine of the Church, he has allowed the children committed to his charge to suck in the poison of this book,—to believe themselves reprobates from the cradle: he has forced them to say—

> If this rebellious heart of mine
> Despise the gracious calls of heaven,
> I may be *hardened by my sin*,
> And never have repentance given.

Instead of being taught that the work of salvation is already accomplished for them, and that all their part is to "continue in the same unto their life's end", they are called upon to begin it at once,—they are called upon to begin it themselves,—they are furiously threatened if they delay this beginning:

> I would not pass another day
> Without this work begun.

How it is to be begun is plentifully repeated:

> Then let me *read and pray*
> While I have life and breath,
> Lest I should be cut off to-day
> And sent to Eternal Death.

To teach children this is "grieving the Holy Spirit of God", whose influences are so strong within them, by telling them that they are absolutely given up and sold under sin,—it is teaching them to trust in themselves for their salvation, and to despise the gift of God; it is throwing away that one precious opportunity which can never be restored; it is arising a vantage ground for all future assaults of their great enemy; it is discouraging all future resistance to temptation; for why should he be resisted who is already in possession? And so the child argues,—I am bad now, and I may as well be bad a little longer. . . . We cannot resist uttering one word of warning, in respect to this very book, to those who call themselves the Evangelical party. Does it not show that there must be something totally and fundamentally wrong in their system, when in a work that to so great a degree forms the mind of their children there is but one reference—and that of the most casual kind—to the Third Person of the ever-Blessed Trinity? In the hymns on the Bible, and on the Sunday, where we should have thought that the writer could hardly fail of referring in the one case to the inspiration, in the other to the descent, of the Holy Ghost, there is not the slightest allusion to either. . . .[1]

Neale here was writing from the experience of his own childhood. As a child he had been repelled by the harsh Calvinistic doctrine in which he had been brought up. One night at the age of eight he had gone to bed " crying those bitter tears that children never forget", in a miserable conviction of his own unconverted condition.[2] It was because of his own bitter experience as a sensitive child that Neale wrote so strongly against some of the evangelical teaching of his early days.

Of his own *Hymns for Children* Neale writes in the article which we have been considering:

> Their recommendation is, that they teach no false doctrine, and that they are written in very easy measures; their great fault, that many of them are intolerably prosaic.[3]

As a great teacher Neale saw the immense importance of hymns in teaching the orthodox faith of the Church to people. He concludes his remarks with the following plea:

> We make no apology for their length, because we feel that the importance of the subject cannot easily be overrated. If Sir Philip Sydney said truly, "Give me the making of a nation's ballads, and I care not who makes its laws",—so with at least equal truth it might be said, "Give me the selection of a Church's Hymns, and I care not who makes,—or rather in the present instance, who has made,— its Articles." No doubt the Puritan depression of the Church of England in the first thirty years of the present century was, in great measure, brought to pass by the heresy of its hymns; may we not, under God, expect the happiest results from Catholic teaching in her future Hymnology? And does it not depend on all and each of us, by the hymns we now employ in our churches, or sanction in our schools, what the future Hymnology of the English Church shall be?[4]

These quotations, which we have made from Neale's article, show his very wide knowledge of the hymns in use in the middle of the nineteenth century, and how clearly he grasped the principles that had to be taken into account in any attempt to

[1] Ibid., pp. 335f.
[2] Towle, *Memoir*, p. 248. See also *Sermons for the Church Year* (New Edition), vol. i (1897), p. 117.
[3] *The Christian Remembrancer*, vol. xviii, p. 337.
[4] Ibid., p. 340.

improve the hymnody of the Church. He refers to these principles in an article two years later in *The Ecclesiologist*. He is writing about the new *Hymnal Noted*:

> Our hymnology is confessedly the weak point of the English Church; heterodoxy in words, and vulgarity in music, will still find their way into Churches, where, with this exception, the Office has ritual propriety, and even dignity. It is not wonderful that of the three requisites to a Hymnal—theology, music, and poetry— scarcely even two, much less all, should be found together. If we escape such heresy as
>
> > When I can read my title clear
> > To mansions in the skies,
>
> or
>
> > Bold shall I stand at that great day,
> > For who aught to my charge shall lay?
> > Completely clothed in Christ alone,
> > And all my filthy garments gone,
>
> then we fall into such poetry as—
>
> > Oh, pluck them out, and be not slow
> > To give my foes a rap.
>
> Or, if we, by great fortune, escape heterodoxy and doggerel, then we have *Sicilian Mariners* or *Cambridge New*.[1]

Neale was well equipped in the matter of theology and poetry for finding the best hymns, and he was ably assisted on the musical side by his friend Thomas Helmore. The various hymnals in use to-day owe much to these two great pioneers of hymn reform.

It is only necessary to add to this that Neale brought his survey of English hymnody up to date in a much later article in *The Christian Remembrancer*, published about three years before his death.[2] One of the books which he discusses here is *Hymns Ancient and Modern*. This was the original edition of 1860. He considers the success which the book had achieved "a very happy circumstance for the prospects of hymnology". He notes however the following defects: (1) the crowd of commonplace hymns; (2) the absence of any Eastern hymns—this of course was remedied in later editions; (3) the absence of some old-fashioned favourites from Watts, Wesley, and others of that stamp (did this show some mitigation of his earlier antipathy to these authors?);

[1] *Letters*, p. 172.
[2] *The Christian Remembrancer*, vol. xlvi (July 1863), p. 105.

(4) the absence, which could not be helped, of some first-rate hymns which had appeared since *Hymns Ancient and Modern*; and (5) needless and often prosaic alterations.[1] Some of Neale's own translations had suffered from this treatment. He also takes *The Salisbury Hymn Book* (1857) to task for not following in places the Latin translations of *Hymnal Noted*. But he is pleased with a number of Bishop Christopher Wordsworth's hymns in *The Holy Year, or Hymns for Sundays and Holidays* (1862), and particularly commends "See the Conqueror mounts in triumph"; "O day of rest and gladness"; and "Hark the sound of holy voices". The first and third he considers to be good imitations of Adam of St Victor, who, to Neale, was the greatest of all Latin poets.[2]

This later article shows how Neale, in spite of his many other activities, kept pace with the latest developments in hymnology right up to the end of his life.

[1] Ibid., pp. 109f.   [2] Ibid., p. 112.

8

Hymns, Ballads, and Carols

IN the previous chapter we saw what Neale thought of the current hymnody of the Church, and the proposals which he made for its reform. We shall now consider the various collections of hymns for which he was responsible, taking them in chronological order.

HYMNS FOR CHILDREN (1842): As we have seen this was Neale's first concern in hymns. He wanted to deliver the children of his day "from the yoke of Watts".[1] This collection consists of thirty-three short hymns, the first nineteen for the different days of the week and different parts of the day, the last fourteen for the different Church seasons. It reached its tenth edition the year after Neale's death.[2] According to his daughter "the spirit that pervades it is the spirit of the Church Catechism, which teaches a baptized child 'heartily' to 'thank our heavenly Father that He hath called me to this state of salvation'".[3] In 1844 a second series of *Hymns for Children* was produced.

Though it does not appear in either of these collections, Neale's facility in writing hymns for children is seen in his hymn, "I am a little Catholic". This was written for the children of St Mary's, Ipswich, on the spot, as they gathered round him to ask how hymns and songs were made.[4]

HYMNS FOR THE SICK (1843): On account of weak health Neale had to spend the winters of 1843–5 in Madeira. At the beginning of this time, when he was only twenty-five, and thought

---

[1] *Letters*, p. 46.
[2] Julian's *Dictionary of Hymnology* (1892), p. 786.
[3] *Letters*, p. 46.
[4] *Collected Hymns, etc. of J. M. Neale* (ed. M. S. Lawson, 1914), p. 398. According to the editor this collection contains all Neale's hymns. It is the best book for studying Neale's work in hymnology.

that he might die of consumption as his father had done, he published this small collection of hymns. The preface shows to how much trouble he went in his attempt to meet the needs of the sick and suffering:

> The following hymns have been written with the wish of setting before the suffering and the sick some of the sources of "strong consolation" which it has pleased our Heavenly Father to lay up for the afflicted in His Holy Church. It is not thoughtlessly that the writer has made choice of (for the most part) uncommon and difficult metres. He knows, both from his own experience and from the testimony of others, how often in illness, particularly in fever, verses written in a very easy and natural metre will run in the mind for hours together, and thus worry, instead of soothing. It was to prevent this effect that he has chosen measures not so likely to recur to, until they weary, the mind.[1]

HYMNI ECCLESIAE E BREVIARIIS QUIBUSDAM ET MISSA-LIBUS GALLICANIS, GERMANIS, HISPANIS, LUSITANIS DESUMPTI (1851): Neale spent many holidays on the Continent, and there he collected from monasteries and libraries many of these hymns. This collection is dedicated to Bishop Torry of St Andrews, who at about this time wanted Neale to become Dean of Perth.[2]

HYMNAL NOTED: PART I (1851), PART II (1856): This collection was sponsored by the Ecclesiological Society, and several articles about it by Neale appeared in *The Ecclesiologist*. Neale was mainly responsible for the words, and the Reverend Thomas Helmore for the music. In an early article Neale writes:

> The proposed Hymnal, it need not be said, will be entirely from ancient sources. The hymns will be taken from those in general use through the Western Church, before the so-called reform of Urban VIII [1568–1644]. And the melody will be that of the best books, and the most correct Churches. The English being of course in the same metre as the Latin, no more alteration will be allowed in the melody than is permitted, in the Latin books, between the different verses of the same hymn.[3]

In a later article Neale justifies this new collection of hymns from the Latin on the following grounds:

---

[1] Ibid., p. 400.
[2] Towle, *Memoir*, p. 182.
[3] *The Ecclesiologist* (new series), vol. viii (Oct. 1850), p. 175.

1. The new collection is based on hymns from the old English office books:

We profess to give the only hymns which we believe the English Church, without the act of a general Synod, to have a right to, those namely of the older English office books, and principally that of Sarum. Now, to say nothing of the many translations afloat from the Paris Breviary with which we, as *English* churchmen, can have nothing to do, except as a matter of curiosity, the hymns that have been translated into English are from the modern Roman Breviary. But the hymns contained in this are—it can never be too often repeated—a mere revision of the older compositions, common for the most part both to Rome and to Sarum, made by the literati of the court of Urban VIII. These men bound themselves down to those classical chains, which the Church had deliberately flung away, and sacrificed beauty, piety, fervour, poetry, to cramp the grand old hymns into the rules of prosody. With much against which we should protest most warmly in Mr Trench's *Sacred Latin Poetry*, we are rejoiced that he has, in sufficiently vivid language, shown "how well nigh the whole grace and beauty and even vigour of the composition has disappeared in the process" of reformation. In fact, the hymns of the modern Roman Breviary, are, emphatically *spoilt*. The translations then of the Roman are not translations of Sarum hymns. Very few of the latter have appeared in English. . . . This then is our first reason, that no translation has yet appeared of our own hymns, and it is with our own hymns that we are concerned. . . .[1]

2. The second reason for a new collection arises out of the question of metre:

But it will truly be said, many of the reformed and unreformed hymns are so nearly the same, that in them, at least, former translations might in great measure be adopted. We come to the second reason which forbids this: the excessive rarity of translations made in the metre of the original; a point to us, of clearly absolute necessity. We open Mr Caswall's *Lyra Catholica*, and, out of the first fifty hymns, one only is in the metre of the original.[2]

Neale always went to great pains in order to get the best possible translation of a hymn. This is shown by the following passage, which appears in the same article:

We should gladly, if we might do so without invidiousness, add a few words on the difficulty of translating Latin hymns. Most people seem to think there is nothing more simple; and, so the general

[1] Ibid. (new series) vol. ix, (old series) vol. xii (February 1851), pp. 11, 12.
[2] Ibid., p. 12.

meaning is preserved, (and that is not always the case) they trouble
themselves with nothing further. But now, to take the first verse,
quoted above, of the *Vexilla Regis*. [The verse to which reference is
made reads as follows:

> Forth comes the standard of the King,
> All Hail, thou Mystery adored!
> Hail, Cross, on which the Life Himself
> Died, and by death our Life restored.]

Probably many persons would think that it was to be read off without
a thought; but may not these questions fairly be asked? Does
Fulget Crucis Mysterium simply mean, The visible Cross with all its
mystic meaning, glitters before us? or, The deep mystery of the
Cross, so long concealed, is now made manifest in full light? . . .
Again, the unreality of the version we quoted above would soon
appear, if a choir following the processional cross were to sing it:

> Forth *comes* the banner of the King.

Must it not manifestly be, "Forth *goes*"? or, as the Hymnal
[i.e. *Hymnal Noted*] has it,

> The Royal banners forward go.[1]

All Neale's work was marked by thoroughness. This was true
of his hymn translations and everything that he did.

In a paper read before the Ecclesiological Society in June 1851,
Neale gives a full account of *Hymnal Noted*:

When the attention of the Ecclesiological Society was first turned
to the subject of Hymnology, we could only act on the same principle which we have endeavoured to carry out in all things, that, if
we were Catholics in the first place, we were English Catholics in
the second. We felt that we could look for our hymns to only one
source, the offices,—or rather to use the proper old, as well as
modern, word,—the *services* of the elder English Church. And of
the various uses of that Church, the ritual of Sarum had so in-
comparably the most authority, that its hymns, we felt, were to be
regarded as our especial inheritance; its hymns, I mean, as contra-
distinguished from later Roman corrections, or rather deformations
of them on the one hand, and on the other from early or mediaeval
hymns, which, however beautiful, were never received in England.
The Sarum Hymnal . . . contains about one hundred and fifty hymns.
Forty of these are translated in the Hymnal before you;—forty or
fifty more, though not of equal importance, may at some future time
appear in its second part;—while the rest are either such as are not
so well adapted to our present circumstances, or in some few
instances, from their poverty or bad taste, undesirable in themselves.[2]

---

[1] Ibid., p. 15.   [2] Ibid. (August 1851), p. 241.

An account of the various authors of the hymns follows—St Ambrose, Prudentius, Sedulius, St Gregory—all "these belong to the first period of Latin hymnology, when the Church was ridding herself of the shackles of quantity, and inventing rhyme".[1] After these are mentioned Venantius Fortunatus (*ob.* 609), St Hrabanus Maurus (856), the Emperor Charlemagne (814), St Fulbert of Chartres (1029), and St Bernard of Clairvaux (1153). Some are by unknown authors.

In describing some of the hymns Neale writes that *Vexilla Regis* (Venantius Fortunatus) is "perhaps the finest hymn (the *Dies Irae*, you know, is not a hymn) which the Western Church possesses", but *Jesu dulcis memoria* is "the sweetest of all hymns".[2]

On the subject of *Sequences* Neale writes as follows:

I need not, perhaps, explain that sequences are distinguished from hymns,—(1) By their use in the Liturgy only; namely between the Epistle and Gospel. (2) By the greater freedon and irregularity of their metre; and by the frequent employment, where they rhyme at all, of prolonged concatenations of double rhymes. (3) By their much greater length. (4) By the difference of their melody: which instead of recurring regularly, recurs partially and irregularly. Without entering into their history, I may just remark, that they appear to have had their rise in the 8th or 9th century; that the northern Churches, as England, Sweden, Brandenburg, Cologne, Utrecht, and more particularly Iceland, were much more partial to them than Italy and Spain; that many Missals, as our own, employed them as regularly as Collect, Epistle, and Gospel; that, at length, there was a perfect mania for composing them; and in the German Missals of the 15th century, there are frequently eight or ten for choice for one festival; till finally, the council of Cologne, in 1536, allowed their omission, and that of Trent ordered it. At present, in the Roman Missal, to the great loss of ritual, four only are retained: the *Dies Irae*, the *Victimae Paschali*, the *Veni Sancte Spiritus*, at Pentecost, and the *Lauda Sion Salvatorem*, at Corpus Christi. The Paris Missal, however, retains many more.[3]

Reference is then made to the two types of Sequence: (1) *Notkerian*, from St Notker (9th century), and (2) *Victorine* from Adam of St Victor (12th century). *Victimae Paschali* is an example of the former, and *Dies Irae* of the latter. Of the last mentioned Neale writes:

The *Dies Irae* is, as I need not observe, by the confession of Catholics and heretics, theologians and poets, the masterpiece of ecclesiastical

[1] Ibid., p. 242.   [2] Ibid., p. 246.   [3] Ibid.

poetry. It is superfluous to remind you how Sir Walter Scott recurred to it on his death bed, and how it gives rise to the most sublime scene in the Faust. The metre, which is unique, the triple hammerstroke, as a German critic calls it, of the triple rhyme, the wonderful simplicity of its words, the fearful sublimity of its ideas, the telling effect of every single word, make it stand alone in its unapproachable glory. But it is worthy of remark, that it by no means occupied the place in the Middle Ages that it does among us. Till the end of the 15th century, it was almost confined to Roman and Italian Missals. . . . With respect to the translation in our book, I am sure its author would agree with me in thinking that our great aim must be to do least badly, what no one can hope to do well. How hopeless it is to produce a satisfactory version, may be seen by the seventy or eighty German versions extant. Yet I cannot but believe that this translation, which manfully grapples with the triple rhyme, is far better than those which quietly drop it, as Mr Caswall's, or even Mr Williams', notwithstanding the far greater ease of that sort of verse.[1]

This translation in *Hymnal Noted* is that of W. T. Irons (1812–1883) and it was made in 1848. It is almost the same as that which appeared later in *Hymns Ancient* and *Modern*. Neale, in spite of his general approval, has some criticisms to make. Of verse three he writes:

The translation in our book gives it, I think, pretty fairly, with one exception of the last word,—"All before the throne it *bringeth*": how different from *coget*! In the next verse, however, no translation that I ever saw seems to have caught the meaning. Ours, as you see, simply asserts two facts, "Death is struck" etc. and "All creation is awaking". But in the Latin, the whole force lies in the word *cum*: *When* creation—or rather, *when* the creature, in the same sense in which our Version speaks of the "*creature* being made subject to bondage not willingly"—*when* the creature shall arise, Death shall be struck with amazement, *stupebit*, namely to see his power over-thrown,—and nature, to see that which by her own laws had returned to dust, thus revivified.[2]

These quotations show the great trouble to which Neale went in order to find the most accurate rendering of the original. As we have seen, he was not the first either to translate the Latin hymns or to attempt to bring them back into use in the Church. Bishop Heber, Bishop Mant, Isaac Williams, John Chandler, Newman, Edward Caswall had all produced translations of a sort. But time has shown that Neale's translations usually have the

[1] Ibid., p. 248.   [2] Ibid., p. 250.

greatest merit and for this reason have won their way and found a permanent place in the hymnology of the Church.

In the introduction to the historical edition of *Hymns Ancient and Modern* (1909), the following notice is taken of *Hymnal Noted*:

> It [*Hymnal Noted*] has left a great mark on this Collection, for some thirty-five versions (including No. 336 now rightly assigned to B. Webb) underlie the corresponding translations here. . . . The *Hymnal Noted* marks the extreme point in the swing of the pendulum in the direction of the Latin office hymns. As a practical hymn-book its contents were too much of one type for it to earn a lasting position; but it impressed once for all on the minds of Churchmen the importance of the old office hymns, and the impression has gone on deepening though the *Hymnal Noted* survives now in only a few places.[1]

Of this work Neale himself says that some of the happiest and most instructive hours of his life were spent in the sub-committee of the Ecclesiological Society appointed for the purpose of bringing out the second part of *Hymnal Noted*.[2] But all these labours were not without their practical difficulties. There was the question of his own personal finances. His income from the wardenship of Sackville College was only £28 a year, and he must have had some private means with which to meet all his commitments. But in June 1852 we find him writing to Webb with reference to *Hymnal Noted*:

> But I very much doubt whether, unless the Society [i.e. the Ecclesiological Society] in some degree pays, I can really afford this.[3]

It is not clear what happened, but it is to be hoped that the Society did make some provision so that he was not out of pocket through the work which he had undertaken.

Then, as the following letter shows, some of the members of the committee could be very awkward:

> Helmore works well, I think, at the Hymnal; but Chambers is very impracticable. He won't correct my hymns; and I don't think he likes my correcting his. What he ought to see is, that, if he publishes another part of the Sarum books, he and we ought to have the same versions of the hymns; and ought to work together. My own theory is this: we ought both to translate all the hymns. Then, I sending a copy of mine, he corrects it by adding what he thinks the best part

---

[1] *Hymns Ancient and Modern* (Historical Edition, 1909), p. ci.
[2] Neale, *Mediaeval Hymns and Sequences* (2nd edn, 1863), p. vii.
[3] *Letters*, p. 192.

of his own; I do the same by him; then we compare the two corrected copies, with the intention of making them the same: if we disagree on any subject, refer to the Committee, whose decision is to be final. But Chambers has a mighty idea of doing everything by himself. It is a great pity. I wish you would try and persuade him to be more conformable: e.g. He has done *Collaudemus Magdalenae*, but I cannot get him to show me his version—nor can I get him to look over mine.[1]

This letter was to Webb, and evidently referred to J. D. Chambers (1810–92), who edited the Sarum Psalter and made various translations of Latin hymns.

But Neale was not to be discouraged or put off by such difficulties as these. To him they were a further challenge to devote his great gifts to the improvement of the hymnody of the Church.

MEDIAEVAL HYMNS AND SEQUENCES (1st Edition 1851; 2nd Edition 1863): This collection consisted of translations of Latin hymns which were not office hymns. In his preface to the second edition, Neale refers to the fact that since the first edition sixty different hymnals had issued from the press, which shows the remarkable output of collections of hymns in the middle of the last century. Neale mentions as most memorable *Hymnal Noted*, *The Sarum Hymnal*, *Hymns Ancient and Modern*, Mr Chope's Collection, and Sir Roundell Palmer's *Book of Praise*. Of his own translations he writes:

> It would be, I think, merely unthankful to Him from Whom all good things come, did I not express my gratitude for the great favour He has given so many of my translations, (both in this and other works) in the English Church: and more especially, "Jerusalem the Golden", "To [*sic*] thee, O dear dear country", "The strain upraise", "Christ is made the sure foundation", and "The Royal Banners". That they have been a good deal altered in their various transcriptions was only to be expected. . . . In some instances I thankfully acknowledge them to be improvements: in some I think that had the reproducers studied the Commentaries of Clichtoveus and Nebrissensis, they would have left the original as it was: I will give an example or two. In the glorious *Ad Coenam Agni providi* the last word of the first line is undoubtedly the nominative case plural:
>
> The Lamb's high banquet *we await*,

as it is in the *Hymnal Noted*. But in most reproductions that line is

[1] Ibid., p. 195.

altered, I suppose from the editors either not seeing or not believing that the adjective applies to ourselves, not to the Lamb.

Again in the same hymn "Cruore ejus roseo" is translated by

And tasting of His roseate Blood.

The epithet is everywhere altered to *Crimson*: because the editors did not see its force. The poet would tell us that, though one drop of our Lord's Blood was sufficient to redeem the world, (Cujus una stilla salvum facere Totum mundum quit ab omni scelere, as St Thomas says) yet out of the greatness of His love to us He would shed all. As every one knows, the last drainings of life-blood are not crimson, but of far paler hue: strictly speaking, *roseate*. Change the word, and you eliminate the whole idea.[1]

In the same preface Neale gives us his ideas about the Latin authors. In his opinion the greatest Latin poet is Adam of St Victor, not only of the medieval period, but of all ages:

It is a magnificent thing to pass along the far-reaching vista of hymns—from the sublime self-containedness of St Ambrose to the more fervid inspiration of St Gregory, the exquisite typology of Venantius Fortunatus, the lovely painting of St Peter Damiani, the crystal-like simplicity of St Notker, the scriptural calm of Godescalus, the subjective loveliness of St Bernard, till all culminate in the full blaze of glory which surrounds Adam of St Victor, the greatest of all. And though Thomas of Celano in one unapproachable Sequence distanced him, and the author, whoever he were, of the *Verbum Dei Deo natum* once equalled him, what are we to think of the genius that could pour forth one hundred Sequences, of which fifty at least are unequalled save by the *Dies Irae*?[2]

Neale, in his interpretation of Adam of St Victor, acknowledges his debt to Dean Trench:

Probably no poet is so hard to translate, from the subtleness of his allusions, the richness of his rhyme, the close way in which he packs his meaning. And I am therefore bound to express my deep gratitude to the first Victorine scholar in England, and probably in Europe, the Dean of Westminster, for his criticisms and alterations.[3]

Neale did not hesitate to give praise where he felt it was due. Before we leave the subject of Neale's translations of Latin hymns we must quote the following story, which shows something of his brilliance in making Latin verses and his facility in translating:

[1] *Mediaeval Hymns and Sequences*, p. vi. ("To thee, O dear dear country" is probably a misprint for "For thee . . .")
[2] Ibid., p. x.
[3] Ibid., pp. x f.

He was invited by Mr Keble and the Bishop of Salisbury to assist them with their new Hymnal, and for this reason he paid a visit to Hursley Parsonage. Mr Keble expressed great pleasure in the remembrance of his visit, saying that he found him so full of cheerfulness and pleasant anecdote. As a specimen, he related that having to go to another room to find some papers he was detained a short time. On his return, Dr Neale said, "Why Keble! I thought you told me, that the *Christian Year* was entirely original!" "Yes", he answered, "it certainly is." "Then how comes this?" And Dr Neale placed before him the Latin of one of Keble's hymns for a Saint's day,— I think it was for St Luke's. Keble professed himself utterly confounded. There was the English, which he knew that he had made, and there too no less certainly was the Latin, with far too unpleasant a resemblance to his own to be fortuitous. He protested that he had never seen this "original", no, not in all his life! etc. etc. After a few minutes, Neale relieved him by owning that he had just turned it into Latin in his absence.[1]

HYMNS OF THE EASTERN CHURCH (1862): Neale's next great work in Hymnology was his introduction to the West of the hymns of the Eastern Church. In this collection "he opened up an unknown storehouse to the West; and, drawing upon it himself, he produced a number of new hymns, partly very free paraphrases of the Greek, and partly original productions inspired by some fragment of a Greek hymn, which in some cases is now no longer traceable".[2]

In the preface to the first edition of this work he wrote:

It is a most remarkable fact, and one which shows how very little interest has hitherto been felt in the Eastern Church, that these are literally, I believe, the only English versions of any part of the treasures of Oriental Hymnology. There is scarcely a first or second-rate hymn of the Roman Breviary which has not been translated: of many we have six or eight versions. The eighteen quarto volumes of Greek Church poetry can only at present be known to the English reader by my little book. Yet surely, if in the future Hymnal of the English Church we are to build an eclectic superstructure on the foundation of the Sarum Book, the East ought to yield its full share of compositions. And hence, I cannot but marvel that the compilers of eclectic Hymnals, such as the (modern) Sarum, the *Hymns Ancient and Modern*, and others, have never turned to this source. Here was a noble field open to them; and to me it is incomprehensible that they should have so utterly neglected it.[3]

[1] G. Moultrie, *Dr Neale*, p. 6. See also Towle, *Memoir*, p. 213.
[2] *Hymns Ancient and Modern* (Historical Edition), p. ci.
[3] Neale, *Hymns of the Eastern Church* (4th edn., 1882), pp. xi f.

This criticism of *Hymns Ancient and Modern* of course refers to the original edition of 1860. In the Appendix, which was added in 1868, several hymns from the Greek were included.

In the same preface Neale goes on to refer to the difficulties which have to be faced in translating from the Greek:

> There are difficulties in the task to which it is as well to revert. Though the superior terseness and brevity of the Latin Hymns renders a translation which shall represent those qualities a work of great labour, yet still the versifier has the help of the same metre; his version may be line for line; and there is a great analogy between the Collects and the Hymns, most helpful to the translator. Above all, we have examples enough of former translation by which we may take pattern. But in attempting a Greek Canon, from the fact of its being in prose,—(metrical Hymns, as the reader will learn, are unknown)—one is all at sea. What measure shall we employ? Why this more than that? Might we attempt the rhythmical prose of the original, and design it to be chanted? Again, the great length of the Canons renders them unsuitable for our churches, as *wholes*. Is it better simply to form centos of the more beautiful passages? or can separate Odes, each necessarily imperfect, be employed as separate Hymns? And above all, we have no pattern or example of any kind to direct our labour. These questions, and many others, have as yet received no reply; but will, in time, no doubt, work out their answer. My own belief is, that the best way to employ Greek Hymnology for the uses of the English Church would be by centos. . . . I trust the reader will not forget the immense difficulty of an attempt so perfectly new as the present, where I have had no predecessors, and therefore could have no master. If I have opened the way for others to do better what I have done imperfectly, I shall have every reason to be thankful. I have kept most of the translations by me for at least the nine years recommended by Horace; and now offer them as a contribution to the hymnology of our own Church.[1]

A second edition of this book appeared in 1862, and a third in 1866. In 1882, sixteen years after Neale's death, the Very Reverend S. G. Hatherly, Archpriest of the Greek Orthodox Church at Bristol, produced a fourth edition with tunes. The music is said to be from Greek and other sources. The tunes, on the whole, are not very attractive, and mostly have not appeared in subsequent hymnals.

Many of Neale's Eastern hymns, however, have been included in later hymnals to different tunes, and are sung to-day. The most notable are perhaps: "The day is past and over"; "Christian,

---

[1] Ibid., pp. xii f.

dost thou see them"; "A great and mighty wonder"; "Come, ye faithful, raise the strain"; and "Stars of the morning, so gloriously bright". Any collection of English hymns to-day, without such hymns as these, would be incomplete.

An Eastern monk of modern times has paid the following tribute to Neale:

> In the Church of England, John Mason Neale was deeply sensitive to the innermost Greek piety, and interpreted it beautifully in his hymnodic translations. He seems to have been, to a large extent, a Greek soul.[1]

SEQUENCES, HYMNS, AND OTHER ECCLESIASTICAL VERSES (1866): Finally we must give some account of Neale's original hymns. Apart from his *Hymns for Children*, and *Hymns for the Sick*, which we have already considered, most of his original hymns are contained in this collection, which was in the press at the time of his death. In the preface dated, "In the Octave of St James" (his patron saint), he writes:

> It had long been my wish, especially when I had occasion to notice the great favour which God has bestowed on my translations from mediaeval hymnology, to collect some of my own Hymns and Sequences as a poor little offering to the Great Treasury. Laid aside, in Spring last, from all active work by a severe and dangerous illness, the wish was more strongly impressed on my mind, and I felt that no kind of composition could be more suitable for one who might soon be called to have done with earthly composition for ever.[2]

The prologue to this collection has a hymn in memory of John Keble, who died a few months before Neale. There are seven sequences, fourteen hymns, and several "ecclesiastical verses", the longest being "The Seven Sleepers of Ephesus". Of the sequences none seems to have found its way into any of the better-known collections of hymns. Of the hymns in this collection the most notable are, "They whose course on earth is o'er", and the Harvest Hymn, "God the Father, Whose Creation". We should also mention the Cattle Plague hymn, "All Creation groans and travails". This hymn was written in the last year of his life, when, on a visit to Cheshire, he was deeply moved by the sight of sick and dying cattle afflicted by some plague. It shows

---

[1] *Orthodox Spirituality*, by a Monk of the Eastern Church (1945), p. ix.
[2] Neale, *Sequences, Hymns, etc.* (1866), p. v.

his deep sympathy with the animal creation. This hymn was included in one of the editions of *Hymns Ancient and Modern*. Amongst the best of Neale's original hymns are two that appear in his *Hymns for Children*, "Christ is gone up; yet ere he passed", and "The earth, O Lord, is one wide field". They appear as embertide hymns in *Hymns Ancient and Modern*. As we have previously noted, Neale saw the value of hymns as a medium of doctrinal teaching.

It now remains to sum up Neale's influence in hymnology. The writer of the introduction to the historical edition of *Hymns Ancient and Modern* pays the following tribute to his original hymns:

> Already we have seen in Dr Neale's work enough to make a reputation for two men [i.e. his translation of Latin and Greek hymns]; but there yet remain his original hymns, half a dozen or more in number in this Collection out of which he might have made a third reputation.[1]

But on the whole Neale's original hymns are not so successful as his translations. It has been said that he always needed some previous fire at which to kindle his torch, and when that was found his success was indeed great.[2] As a translator of Latin hymns he is surely supreme. No other translations are so satisfying. One only has to compare his translations with those of Caswall, or in more recent times with those of the late Monsignor Ronald Knox, to realize how vastly superior is the work of Neale in this respect. As examples of this, the three versions of the Whitsuntide Sequence *Veni, Sancte Spiritus* may be compared (*English Hymnal*, 155—Neale; *Hymns A. & M.* [*Standard*], 156—Caswall; *Westminster Hymnal*, 64—Knox); also the two versions of *Jesu dulcis memoria* (*Hymns A. & M.* [*Standard*], 177, 178). It is noteworthy that the *English Hymnal*, in most of the office hymns, has Neale's version in preference to that of Caswall or someone else. In Julian's *Dictionary of Hymnology* Dr Overton writes:

> He had all the qualifications of a good translator. He was not only an excellent classical scholar in the ordinary sense of the term, but he was also positively steeped in mediaeval Latin. . . . Again Dr Neale's exquisite ear for melody prevented him from spoiling the

---

[1] *Hymns Ancient and Modern* (Historical Edition), p. ci.
[2] *Collected Hymns, etc. of J. M. Neale*, p. v.

rhythm by too servile an imitation of the original, while the spirited-
ness which is the marked feature of all his poetry preserved that
spring and dash which is so often wanting in a translation.[1]

In fact it is true to say that his translations read as originals.
Though he was at great pains to bring out every shade of the
meaning of the original, yet there is little to show that they are
translations.

We conclude this brief survey of Neale's work in hymnology
with two final quotations, one from Mrs Towle and the other
from his daughter:

> All his hymns are absolutely free from sentimentality either of
> thought or diction. There is a sense of pressing forward, a hurrying
> towards a goal, and notes of encouragement to cheer the toilworn
> traveller on his way. As Dr Littledale observed there was a masculine
> strength in his writings, the more remarkable as they were so often
> addressed to women, and the same observation may be applied with
> equal truth to his hymns.[2]

Hymnology can hardly be considered at the present time the "weak
point" in the English Church, and it would be difficult to overestimate John Mason Neale's work in this particular line. Perhaps
his hymns have a more widely spreading influence than any of his
other writings, whether it be his sermons, his Commentary, his
"History of the Eastern Church", or his "Church Tales". There is
probably no modern hymnal, Anglican or Nonconformist, where
his hymns are not, and in some collections they form a very large
proportion. For instance, in one of the editions of "Hymns Ancient
and Modern", not less than *one-eighth* of the hymns and translations—
61 out of 473—came from his pen. In the "English Hymnal" more
than *one-tenth* are his: 72 out of 656. In this later book it is gratifying
to find that, as a rule, his translations are given word for word as he
wrote them, and that therefore at the great Church Pageant this
year (1909) his translations, unaltered, were used of the glorious
hymns, *Urbs Beata, Angulare Fundamentum*, and *Dies Irae*.[3]

Mary Lawson here is wrong about *Dies Irae*, which was
translated not by her father, but by W. T. Irons. The fact that it is
included in *Hymnal Noted*, most of which was by her father,
probably made her think that it was his. Her judgement on her
father's influence in Anglican hymnology is largely true, but it

---

[1] Julian's *Dictionary of Hymnology*, p. 787.
[2] Towle, *Memoir*, pp. 215f.
[3] *Letters*, p. 175. *Hymns Ancient and Modern Revised* (1950) has 56 hymns of
Neale; *Songs of Praise* (1932) has 19; *The Westminster Hymnal* (1939) has 9; and *The
Methodist Hymn Book* (1933) has 14.

should be noticed that the compilers of *Hymns Ancient and Modern* rejected his idea of a largely ancient hymn book with a few good English hymns. *Hymns Ancient and Modern* in its various editions includes many hymns by eighteenth-century authors, such as Watts, the Wesleys, and Newton. Neale himself would probably have rejected most of them. But the importance of Neale's work on the ancient hymns of the Church is indeed difficult to overestimate.

Though, strictly speaking, ballads and carols do not come under the heading of hymnology, it is convenient that in this chapter we should make some mention of Neale's work in this connection, especially as his work with carols was so important.

SONGS AND BALLADS FOR THE PEOPLE (1843); SONGS AND BALLADS FOR MANUFACTURERS (1844); A MIRROR OF FAITH (1845): As we have seen, Neale had a profound interest in the working conditions of the ordinary people. The state of the poor and under-privileged classes was much upon his conscience. For this reason he had carried on his campaign against pews. For this reason he had founded the Society of St Margaret. We find this same concern for the poor in some of his early poetic work. One of his earliest published works was *Songs and Ballads of the People*, published in 1843, when he was only twenty-five. This collection consists of sixteen ballads on such subjects as: "The Church of England"; "The Teetotallers"; "The Church-Rate"; "Village Politicians"; "Why are you a Dissenter?" and (perhaps inevitably) "Pews". The object of these ballads would seem to be to encourage loyalty to the Church, and to counteract subversive movements against her. The first and last stanzas of the first ballad, "The Church of England", are as follows:

> The good old Church of England!
>   With Her Priests through all the land,
> And Her twenty thousand churches,
>   How nobly does She stand!
> Dissenters are like mushrooms,
>   That flourish but a day;
> Twelve hundred years, through smiles and tears,
>   She hath lasted on alway!

> God bless the Church of England!
> The poor man's Church is She;
> We were nourish'd at Her bosom,
> We were fondled at Her knee.
> God bless the Church of England!
> The good, the true, the brave!
> She baptis'd us in our cradle;
> She shall bear us to our grave.

Neale never had much sympathy with Dissenters, and he would certainly never have agreed with the view that the Church of England was only for the upper and middle classes.

Here are the first and last stanzas of his ballad on Pews:

> Come, list to me, neighbours! come, list to my song!
> Our Parson is right, and the parish is wrong:
> He wants to take down all the pews, as you know;
> He has plenty of reasons, and good ones, to show;
> And I'll make them so clear, that there's none shall refuse
> To join him in crying—Away with the pews!
>
> And then rich and poor, as the way was of yore,
> Will have all the same seats, free and open once more:
> 'Twas a rare wicked system; but now it has passed,
> And our country has found out its mischief at last:
> Open seats in all churches! and none must refuse,
> FOR ENGLAND HAS SAID IT—Away with the pews!

In the following year appeared *Songs and Ballads for Manufacturers*. A note on the first page of this publication dated 15 January 1844, Madeira, says:

> The aim of the following verses is to set forth good and sound principles in metaphors, which may, from their familiarity, come home to the hearts of those to whom they are addressed.

In this collection there are thirteen ballads with such titles as: "The Silk Throwsters", "The Glassblowers", "The Figure-Weavers", "The Cotton-Spinners", "The Iron-Founders", "The Miners", "The Engine Drivers". That Neale knew all the technical terms in connection with these employments is clear from his footnotes. It is remarkable how well informed he was about any subject on which he wrote. He knew all the details of the various jobs described, and drew appropriate lessons from them. The following are the first two and last two stanzas of "The Engine Drivers":

Water and flame to agreement came,
  And a solemn league they swore,
To work such speed and to do such deed
  As never was done before:
To be friends to Time, to be foes to space,
  To mingle their rival powers,
And at giants' pace, in a giant's race,
  To be slaves to us and ours.

The sign is made, the word is said,
  And the boiler coughs and hoots,
And taught to go at the first right slow,
  The long line onward shoots:
Till with valves that rattle quick, and with steam that
      volumes thick,
And with *buffers* each from other far apart,
While the *sleepers* quake below, and the wheels like
      lightning go,
Through the tunnel and the bridge we dart.

The hour will be past if we pause at last,
  So faster, if faster may be;
The clouds that fly through the summer sky
  Are not so swift as we;
There's a whir in the trees when we pass like the
      breeze,
  As if all we had done were too slow,
And for breath we must gasp, and the tender-rails
      we clasp,
As a mile in a minute we go.

We may hear the bell of our coming tell
  A long long league away;
And the pleasant field to the town must yield,
  Ere we end our toil to-day:
For life and for limb one thought to Him
  Of thankfulness we give,
Who guides us aright in our whirlwind flight,
  When we could not go wrong and live!

A Mirror of Faith was produced in 1845 with the subtitle *Lays and Legends of the Church of England*. In this collection the following from "The Good Old Times of England" reveals something of Neale's hopes for the Church of England of his day:

And many an earnest prayer ascends
from many a hidden spot;
And England's Church is Catholic,
though England's self be not!
England of Saints! The hour is nigh
—far nigher may it be
Than yet I deem, albeit that day
I may not live to see—
When all thy commerce, all thy arts,
and wealth, and power, and fame,
Shall melt away—at thy most need—
like wax before the flame;
Then shalt thou find thy truest strength
thy martyrs' prayers above,
Then shalt thou find thy truest wealth
their holy deeds of love;
And thy Church, awaking from her sleep,
come glorious forth at length,
And in sight of angels and of men
display her hidden strength:
Again shall long processions sweep
through Lincoln's minster pile:
Again shall banner, cross and cope
gleam thro' the incensed aisle;
And the faithful dead shall claim their part
in the Church's thankful prayer,
And the daily sacrifice to God
be duly offered there;
And Tierce, and Nones, and Matins,
shall each have their holy lay;
And the Angelus at Compline
shall sweetly close the day.

England of Saints! the peace will dawn,
—but not without the fight;
So, come the contest when it may,
And God defend the right!

CAROLS FOR CHRISTMASTIDE (1853); CAROLS FOR
EASTERTIDE (1854): Neale first set his hand to carols when
at the request of Messrs Masters and Co., the publishers, in 1851,
he wrote an Easter and a Christmas carol set to ancient melodies
—"Joy to thee, joy in thee", and "Joy and gladness".[1]

In 1853 Novello and Co. published *Carols for Christmastide,*
and in the following year *Carols for Eastertide.* According to *The
Oxford Book of Carols* "this was the first recognition since old

[1] *Memoir*, p. 210b.

times of the carol apart from Christmas".[1] But as we saw above Neale had published an Easter carol two years before this. In these two collections Neale was responsible for the words, and the Reverend Thomas Helmore for the music.

The importance of these collections, as Dr Erik Routley and others have pointed out, lies in the fact that they were based on a rare book which had been brought from Sweden and given to Neale and Helmore. The full title of the book was *Piae Cantiones Ecclesiasticae et Scholasticae, veterum Episcoporum, in Inclyto Regno Sueciae passim usurpatae.* Mr G. J. R. Gordon, her Majesty's Envoy and Minister at Stockholm, was responsible for bringing the book to this country and showing it to Neale and Helmore. Neale in his preface to his collection says that *Piae Cantiones* was originally published for the use of the Lutheran Communion in Sweden in 1582. He goes on to say: "Neither Words nor Music, however, were in that work changed from earlier sources; and they occur in the libraries of Germany, England, and France with no other difference than traditionary repetition and popular variations would naturally introduce."[2]

Piae Cantiones consisted of seventy-three Latin hymns and carols set to their proper melodies. Dr Routley shows that the tunes of this collection are important because they have been used to a large extent in later English carol books. "We have many tunes, but few words, from *Piae Cantiones*."[3]

Neale's most popular carol, though rather hackneyed to-day, was undoubtedly "Good King Wenceslas". The words, which are original and not a translation, are based upon a Bohemian legend. Neale relates this legend in a little book dedicated to his eldest daughter, Agnes, in 1849, and called *Deeds of Faith*. In the preface to this book he refers to it as "a legend of extreme beauty".[4] The tune of course is taken from *Piae Cantiones*. The carol itself, in spite of its popularity with many people, has had its critics amongst the more learned. Dr Percy Dearmer referred to its "rather confused narrative". E. Duncan called it "doggerel", and A. H. Bullen condemned it as "poor and commonplace to the last degree".[5] Dr Routley, however, has something to say for it:

---

[1] *The Oxford Book of Carols* (1928), p. xvi.
[2] Neale and Helmore, *Carols for Christmastide* (1853). Preface to full music edition.
[3] Erik Routley, *The English Carol* (1958), p. 192.
[4] Neale, *Deeds of Faith* (1849), p. ix.
[5] *The Oxford Book of Carols*, p. 271.

"I am unable to see what is wrong with 'Good King Wenceslas' as a sociable carol. It lacks pious unction, and looking at the nineteenth century productions that have it, we may be thankful for that."[1] Neale certainly could never be accused of pious unction. If he had ever found himself in the position of the good king, he would surely have acted in much the same way himself.

Neale not only wrote and translated carols; he organized carol parties himself at East Grinstead. When his collections of carols had been published, a choir of men and boys met once or twice a week in the hall of Sackville College to practise them. On Christmas and Easter eves the party went forth into the town with lanterns to sing. His son, Vincent, who as a boy took part in the singing, described it as follows: "The chief stand was in the double main street, and was a picturesque sight, with the glare of torches, and the players of the string and wind instruments. The baker played the bass fiddle. All formed in a large circle with the singers inside the ring. The warden was always present. . . ."[2]

Neale's daughter relates how on one occasion a certain member of the choir, who was a teetotaller and a vegetarian, asked that in "Good King Wenceslas" the king's command:

> Bring me flesh and bring me wine

might be altered to

> Bring me milk and bring me bread.

The line to rhyme with this alteration was presumably to be

> Thou and I will see him fed.

Needless to say the writer of the ballad entitled "The Teetotallers" did not comply.[3]

---

[1] Routley, op. cit., p. 193.
[2] Article by Vincent Neale in *St Margaret's Quarterly* (U.S.A.), Summer 1955 (this is the magazine of the American branch of the Society of St Margaret), a reprint of an article which appeared in 1918.
[3] *Letters*, p. 281. The following are the first three verses of "The Teetotallers":

> And so the Teetotallers meet here to-day!
> Well! they talk very big, and they look very gay;
> And they tease me to join them from morning till night;
> But first I've one question, and that's—Is it right?

> They talk a great deal about taking the vow,
> How they once used to drink, and are temperate now;
> Well! I can't see the virtue, or glory at least
> Of promising not to turn into a beast.

Or supposing there were,—they have taken before
All the vows they now take, ay, and very much more:
Not from drinking alone, but all sin to abstain;
When they first were baptis'd—why take it again?

As with hymns, so with carols, the English-speaking world
owes much to Neale's work.

9

Reunion and Rome

ONE result of the Catholic revival in the Church of England
in the last century was that church people were made to
think seriously of what was meant by the Holy Catholic
Church. This article of the Creed had been sadly neglected for
over a century. The Tractarians recalled men to its vital truth,
and insisted that the Church of England was a true part of the
historic Catholic Church. From this fact it was forced upon
churchmen to consider the relationship of the Church of England
to the rest of Catholic Christendom, and also to study the problem
of the unity of the Church. In this part of our study we shall
consider Neale's work in connection with the relationship of the
Church of England to other Catholic Communions. We should
state here that Neale had no great interest in Nonconformity.
The Church of England had nothing to learn from it. His
attitude is expressed in a letter written in 1842:

> I had a long argument with Wackerbarth, the Romanist, and never
> felt before, so much, how invincible we Anglicans are, if we will
> only abjure all common cause with Protestants.[1]

To-day many would consider Neale's attitude to be intolerant;
but people in Victorian England often were intolerant, probably
because they had for the most part stronger convictions than the
people of to-day. Neale had been brought up in a strict evangelical
home with a strong Calvinistic emphasis. His sensitive, poetic
nature revolted against it, and when Catholic truth was presented
to him, he grasped it with delight. He was determined to show
that the Church of England was the traditional Catholic Church
of the land. Nonconformity to him simply meant dullness,
negation, and individualism. He had, however, friends amongst
Nonconformist ministers. The Reverend G. Moultrie relates

[1] *Letters*, p. 41.

how he helped a certain Independent minister who was in difficulties with his people, and how he had a warm admirer in the person of a Presbyterian minister, who used to resort to him for the loan of books. When this same minister fell ill, he was given the hospitality of Sackville College.[1]

We shall first of all in this chapter consider Neale's attitude towards the Church of Rome. Then in the two following chapters we shall see how he worked for a better understanding by Anglicans of the Eastern Church and of the so-called Jansenist Church in Holland, now part of the Old Catholic Communion.

At the beginning of this part of our study it is necessary to emphasize Neale's concern for the unity of the Church. There are many references to it in his writings. But he knew that there were no short cuts to unity, and that much prayer was necessary. In his preface to *Voices from the East* he writes:

> And now I pray God to accept this volume as a mite thrown into the treasure-house of preparation for Union. The Union of the Three Churches, that second and even more glorious Pentecost, we cannot hope to see; but in the meantime, amidst all the obloquy, and disputes, and suspicions, and hard words of this generation, it is a blessed and consoling dream, which some day will, most assuredly, become a reality.[2]

Here of course by "the Three Churches" he means the Church of Rome, the Eastern Church, and the Church of England.

The Reverend George Williams, who was responsible for editing and publishing Neale's unfinished history of the Patriarchate of Antioch, in his introduction to this work refers to Neale's zeal for the sacred cause of reunion, and his hope for "the gradual approximation and ultimate reconciliation of the long-estranged families of Catholic Christendom, on the basis of a better mutual understanding". Williams goes on to say: "And although he was not permitted to see the consummation of his ardent desires, yet his latter years were gladdened by the unmistakeable evidences of a wider and constantly increasing interest —both at home and abroad—in the cause of a reunited Christendom, which had been for many years the day-dream of a small and uninfluential section of Anglican Churchmen."[3]

---

[1] G. Moultrie, *Dr Neale*, pp. 3f.
[2] Neale, *Voices from the East* (1859), p. vii.
[3] Neale, *A History of the Holy Eastern Church, The Patriarchate of Antioch* (ed. George Williams, 1873), pp. ix, x.

With reference to Neale's work on the Eastern Church, Sister Miriam wrote: "Re-union was now, and henceforth to the end, the object of his hopes, and desires, and labours. To say, to write, to do anything towards the fulfilment of our Lord's prayer, 'That they all may be one', no difficulty was too great to be encountered."[1] We thus see his deep concern for reunion.

We now pass on to consider Neale's views about the Roman Communion. They do not seem to have changed much as the years went by. Most of his friends only knew Roman Catholicism as it was in England. He knew it in a country outside England. As we have seen in a previous chapter, at the age of twenty-five he went to Madeira on account of his health, and spent three winters there. Though he had a great interest in the Church of the island, attending many of the services and making friends with some of the priests, he found much to criticize. In a letter to Webb dated 20 February 1843 he writes:

> This place, in an Ecclesiastical point of view, is the most discouraging and regrettable that you can conceive. As to the Church, I fear it is in a most deplorable state. I dined on Saturday with a Mr Monro, who has paid some attention to the subject, and, though a Protestant, is not a bigoted one—so this opinion may go for something. Indeed, the look of the thing may shew you that there is something wrong. Processions not allowed; the Church is not open; and though I have kept a pretty strict watch I have not seen High Mass once. . . . In the Island newspaper, *O Defensa*, I saw an article on the decay of the Catholic faith, which they attribute to the vicious lives of the clergy. . . .[2]

In Madeira Neale met Count Montalembert, the French Roman Catholic liberal historian. He and Neale seem to have taken to one another and they had many discussions together. Montalembert was trying to do in France to some extent what the Cambridge Camden Society was trying to do in England. He was delighted with Neale's *Hierologus*, and especially with the parts relating to abbeys.[3] He was an ultramontanist, and tried to win over Neale to his views, but the latter was quite unshaken by any arguments which the Count put forward. In fact Montalembert seems to have been rather annoyed with Neale at one stage, and went so

[1] *Memoir*, p. 9b.
[2] *Letters*, pp. 49, 50.
[3] Ibid., p. 70. *Hierologus*, published in 1843, was an account of some church tours made by Neale and his friends.

far as to accuse Anglo-Catholics of being "the worst enemies of the Church, more so than infidels themselves".[1] In spite of these differences, however, the two continued to see one another as long as Neale was in Madeira.

During the next two years the Catholic movement in England was reaching a crisis. On 9 October 1845 Newman was received into the Roman Communion. Many followers of the Tractarians were gravely disturbed by this, but Neale remained calm and quite unshaken. Again and again in his letters and sermons his firm conviction that the Church of England is a true part of the historic Catholic Church is apparent. Never in the whole of his life is there the slightest hint of a possible secession to Rome on his part, and there is no doubt that both at the time of the Newman secessions, and at the time of the Gorham Case, he saved many from going that way. As Mother Kate wrote: "Dr Neale himself had not the very slightest Roman tastes or tendencies; no man less."[2]

When Benjamin Webb was worried about rumours of Newman's possible secession, Neale wrote to him from Madeira in a letter dated 26 November 1844:

> I hope and believe that Newman will not leave us; but I should not despair if he did. My sheet anchor of hope for the English Church is, that you cannot point out a single instance of a heretical or schismatical body, which after apparent death awoke to life.[3]

A few weeks later on 31 December Webb again wrote a somewhat panicky letter to Neale:

> Now we fear for the worst. I want you to look this in the face: that in twelve months, if we live, we may perchance be in the Roman Church. We must be prepared for some such emergency; for who would think of non-juring?[4]

Neale's reply unfortunately is not preserved, but he would have had little sympathy with Webb's vacillation. Eleven months later, about a month after Newman's secession, on 8 November 1845 he wrote to Webb:

> As to Newman's book [i.e. *Essay on the Development of Christian Doctrine*] I am so thoroughly and morally persuaded of the

---

[1] Towle, *Memoir*, p. 80.
[2] Mother Kate, *Memories of a Sister of St Saviour's Priory* (1903), p. 35.
[3] *Letters*, p. 80.
[4] Ibid., p. 81.

defensibility of our position, that if I were to feel shaken by its beginning, I would shut up the book. I cannot express to you the firmness of my conviction. It seems to grow upon me the more the others waver.[1]

In another letter, dated Advent Eve 1845, he wrote:

... I am more than ever inclined to go with Hope's theory, and believe that the first generation of reformers may perhaps be absorbed by Rome: but that the second will remain in our Church and renovate it. ... I am quite sure that if we don't desert ourselves, God will not desert us. If you all go, I shall stay. If Andrewes is not saved (who had far less reason than we have to remain) there are so few that will be, that really, it cannot matter whether one goes or not.[2]

These letters show Neale's calmness at the time of Newman's secession, when others were wringing their hands and shedding tears.

Five years later, when the Gorham Judgement shook the Church of England, he again remained as firm as a rock, and saved many from going the same way as Manning. His pamphlet, *A Few Words of Hope in the Present Crisis of the English Church,* had a great stabilizing influence. In the Gorham Judgement the Judicial Committee of the Privy Council had in effect decreed that a priest who did not believe in baptismal regeneration might hold office in the Church of England. Neale took the line that the Church was not in any way committed by the decision of a secular court. The ultimate appeal was to the Convocations of the Church, which at that time were not allowed to meet. The formularies of the Church were perfectly sound on the doctrine in question, and the judgement of a secular court could not affect it. At about that time Neale wrote to his former tutor, the Reverend William Russell:

First let me assure you, that however much I deplore the decision of the Privy Council, I am not shaken in fidelity to our Church; and if I was, I should not go to Rome, but to Scotland.[3]

In a later letter he quotes evidently with some amusement Manning's view of the Scottish Episcopal Church as a possible refuge for English Catholics: "He [Dodsworth—Vicar of Christ Church, Albany Street] told me that Manning said of the Scotch Church—'We got out of the ship into the boat at the Reformation, but I am not going to get out of the boat into the tub'."[1] Neale himself had no such qualms. He was quite unmoved by the papal claims, and from his profound knowledge of church history considered that they were wrong. He objected to the Roman additions to the traditional doctrines of the Church. He had little sympathy with those who deserted the Church of England for the Roman Communion. What he thought about their action is shown in his sermon on "Secession" to the Sisters. The following extracts from this sermon give some idea where Neale stood in this matter:

> We, you know, descend directly from the old Church of England. We are the spiritual children of St Osmund, St Thomas of Canterbury, St Richard of Chichester, St Felix of Suffolk. A very few generations, and I can trace my orders to our great martyr of Canterbury. The Roman Church in England has its orders from Spain. You may not know that, at the accession of Elizabeth, the Bishops who would not conform ordained no successors. The Roman Catholics in England for five years attended our churches, and received our Sacraments. Then,—not till then—Pius V excommunicated and deposed the queen; but not for sixty years had the Romanists any Bishop. About 1620 one Dr Bishop, calling himself Bishop of Chalcedon, was sent over: he had been consecrated in Spain: and from him modern Romanists derive their orders. Then: either that Church of Saints has come to an end, or it exists in us.[2]

He refers to the additional Roman doctrines as follows:

> What then do I see? On the one hand, the English Church teaching three or four doctrines less clearly and plainly than I could wish— dimly, if you will, and indistinctly—but teaching them still: on the other, Rome teaching three or four doctrines which Bernard, which Thomas Aquinas, which Rupert, which Bonaventura called blasphemous, and forcing them on us. Had I no other duty to stay where I am, am I not therefore safer? Verily, yes. Listen to me, my Sisters. For four years now past I have taught you weekly, sometimes almost daily, from mediaeval writers; what they said to their Sisters, I, without alteration, say to you. When I say without alteration, I mean without doctrinal alteration. There I call God to witness, neither by way of addition or subtraction, do I remember, in those five hundred sermons I have preached to you, to have made a single change. Well; then we hold now what they held, exactly and literally.
>
> Now mark me: a Roman Priest could not do so. His sermons, if he did, would be at least branded as without unction, probably

---

[1] Ibid., p. 145.
[2] *Sermons Preached in a Religious House* (1st series), vol. i, p. 181.

termed heretical, because he would not speak of St Mary as the channel of all grace. The Sisters of this day are not taught what Bernard taught—are taught what Bernard protested against. You know how he wrote against what he calls the blasphemy of the Immaculate Conception. And not only that: that dear Litany which he wrote, and which we say daily,—how is it characterized by modern Romanists? A criticism the other day termed it *profane*, as applying to our Lord the title, "Star of the Sea", which, they say, ought to be confined to St Mary! What would he, what would those mediaeval Convents of his, have said to such a doctrine?[1]

He speaks very strongly against the Roman practice of Communion in one kind:

Then, how miserable to be deprived for ever of the Chalice of which He said, "Drink ye all of it!" You know, my Sisters, how I grieve from my very soul that His greatest gift has been so little esteemed, so much dishonoured among us; you know that I would sacrifice anything, lay down anything to see, what I hope some day will be,— the Eucharistic teaching of our Church—I will not say, more true— but more distinct, or rather more true, because more distinct. But, were I in the Roman Communion, what agony it would be to see the Chalice so abused! to know what that dear Lord shed out of His most Precious Side, that I might drink it; that He said, "Drink ye all of it"; that he still says, "Come drink of My Wine that I have mingled"; and to have the Church interpose, and say, "No; I forbid it". You may not know the story of the Bishop of Exeter, Ralph de Queval, in the thirteenth century, when the corruption was first authoritatively taught in England, who said, "Whatever be the consequence of my disobedience, I never will so incestuously maim the Sacrament." And, during his life time he never did. . . . And we ought to remember too, the great Eastern Church, with its seventy millions of Christians, never ceases to protest against the maimed Sacrament and the corrupted Sacrifice![2]

It is clear from passages like these that Neale was no Romanizer. He had much to criticize in the Roman system. Whilst he longed for the ultimate union of the whole Church, he looked elsewhere than to Rome for the first stage in the movement towards reunion, as we shall see in the following chapters.

In the sermon quoted above reference is made to the doctrine of the Immaculate Conception. Neale himself had no objection to the doctrine as such. Some passages in his sermons seem to show his belief in it. But he objected strongly to its being made a dogma of the Church. On 23 October 1854 he wrote to Webb:

[1] Ibid., pp. 182f.
[2] Ibid., pp. 186f. The whole of this sermon should be read to appreciate Neale's attitude to Roman additions to the Creeds.

What a shocking thing will this Decree *Urbi et Orbi* be, when it really comes out! I have no particular feeling against the dogma myself; but for the Pope to make it thus necessary to salvation is really too bad. I think that every step modern Rome takes is more and more against her. In fact, if we are to be finally lost for not going with her, it is a very hard case indeed.[1]

Neale died four years before the Vatican Council of 1870, and so what he thought about the dogma of Papal Infallibility is not known. From his attitude towards the Roman claims it is clear that he would have greatly regretted it. To him it would have done nothing towards healing the divisions of the Church. It would only have made for the widening of the breaches between Rome and Canterbury, and the East and the West.

Before we conclude this chapter we must note an interesting fact about Neale's liturgical practices. In spite of his strong anti-papalism and deep Eastern sympathies, he adopted certain views and practices which are Western rather than Eastern. He taught the Western theory of consecration in the Eucharist.[2] He introduced Benediction with the Blessed Sacrament in St Margaret's Oratory in 1859 (as we have seen, he started a daily Eucharist in 1856, and Reservation in 1857). He had the Stations of the Cross in the Oratory in 1858, if not earlier.[3] Neale would be perfectly at home in any Anglo-Catholic church to-day, whereas Keble, Isaac Williams, and other Tractarians might feel a little strange. Neale, whilst firmly opposing the papal claims, adopted these Western liturgical practices, because he regarded the Church of England as part of the Western Church, and therefore within the Western tradition. He considered that the Church of England should be loyal to her own pre-Reformation traditions, which were not specifically papal. Furthermore, as we have seen, he had a deep sympathy with the poor, the simple, and the underprivileged, and was a born teacher. Therefore he did not hesitate to use aids which had been tried in another part of the Church in order to bring home to people the truths of the Catholic Faith.

[1] *Letters*, p. 230.
[2] Neale, *Sermons on the Blessed Sacrament* (new edn), p. 174.
[3] Neale, *Sermons for Feast Days*, p. 66.

IO

The Holy Eastern Church

THERE had of course been contacts since the Reformation between the Church of England and the Eastern Patriarchates long before the start of the Oxford Movement,[1] but one result of the Catholic revival in the nineteenth century was a renewed interest in the Eastern as well as the Roman Church. It is interesting to note that Neale's thoughts turned towards the Eastern Church when his friend Webb and others were greatly worried by the Roman question at the time of Newman's secession.

Not many men would undertake the writing of a history of the whole of the Eastern Church, but Neale was always ready to apply himself to tasks which other men would have deemed impossible. According to Sister Miriam his two most important literary works were his *Commentary on the Psalms*, and his *History of the Holy Eastern Church*.[2] Both works were started in Madeira and carried on through the rest of his life, but he did not live to see the completion of either.

Early in 1843 Neale had written to Webb:

I think I might undertake a very favourite plan of mine; a history of the Eastern Church to the present time—perhaps only from the great schism of East and West.[3]

But when he settled down to the task, he evidently decided to write the history of the various patriarchates from the beginning.

In a later letter he wrote of some of the difficulties which he was finding:

[1] For a summary of these contacts see article "Reunion" in *Dictionary of English Church History*, ed. Ollard, Crosse, and Bond (3rd edn, 1948), pp. 526f.
[2] *Memoir*, pp. 6b f.
[3] Towle, *Memoir*, p. 99.

I have been at our history tooth and nail, principally working at Constantinople; but I have worked off this chapter, and I wish to have your opinion of it. You must be merciful in your judgement; you only see the result, but don't know the difficulties—Catholics contradicting Protestants, Jacobites contradicting both; Coptic names so altered that they are hardly the same in two books. I was quite put out till I discovered that David, of Geddes, and Onadingial, of La Croze, were the same person. . . . I never shall have courage for this without your help. I don't care how much of it, so you take *some*. After all, it will be perfectly new to ninety-nine readers out of a hundred.[1]

Some months later he wrote:

I find the Greek history pleasanter every day. But it is not an easy thing, and the worry from the fear of making a mistake used at first to be quite painful. It is, however, a very good exercise. Especially I find the having to define in a few brief words, the early heresies, very improving to one's divinity. . . .[2]

Neale took all his work very seriously, and was always at pains to get his facts right and to give as accurate an account as possible of any historical event. In one of his history books for children he referred to the anxiety which the writing of the book had caused him.[3]

The first two volumes of his work on the Eastern Church were published in 1847 under the title of *A History of the Holy Eastern Church—The Patriarchate of Alexandria*. These volumes took him four years to complete and must have entailed a vast amount of research. In the preface to the first volume he gives his main authorities as follows:

1. Michael Le Quien (1661–1773), the French Dominican Father, whose treatise *De Patriarchatu Alexandrino* is contained in the second volume of his *Oriens Christianus*. Neale praises this work, but says that it is weakened by the fact that the author did not know Arabic.

2. Eusèbe Renaudot (1646–1720), the French orientalist and liturgist. He was a member of the Académie Française. He was in minor orders in the Church, and had connections with the Jansenists. The title of his work was *History of the Jacobite Patriarchs of Alexandria*. We are told that this history extends from the time of St Mark to the year 1703:

[1] Ibid., p. 99.
[2] Ibid., p. 100.
[3] Neale, *A History of the Church for the Use of Children* (1852), p. iv.

The immense learning of Renaudot, his acquaintance with nearly thirty languages, his devotion to Eastern literature, and the advantage which he enjoyed in being able to consult the unrivalled collection of Manuscripts in the King's Library at Paris, have rendered his work, so far as it goes, more complete than probably any other scholar could have made it.

But at the same time this work "has all the faults of Renaudot; it is insufferably long, tedious and confused; learning is wasted in the discussion of points known to all the world; and the thread of history broken and taken up again in the most perplexing manner imaginable".[1]

3. Wansleb, a Dominican missionary in Egypt. This work, however, had continual inaccuracies, and "the scanty information which it furnishes on any subject, renders it nearly useless, except for occasional reference".

4. John Baptist Sollerius, a Jesuit. The title of his work is *Chronological Series of Alexandrian Patriarchs*. It was not, however, of great value, because the author was not acquainted with the Eastern languages and had access to no manuscripts.

In addition to these general sources there were many others which dealt with only a part of the period under consideration, e.g. Eutychius for the Catholic Patriarchs of Alexandria, Elmacinus for the Jacobite Patriarchs, and the Mahometan, Makrizi.

Whilst in Madeira, Neale found the library at Funchal with its valuable edition of the Fathers very useful for his work, but it was not enough to answer all his questions. He had to make inquiries further afield. He was in constant correspondence with his friend Benjamin Webb and his old adviser Dr Mill.[2] He acknowledges his debt to both in his preface.

On 11 January 1844 he wrote from Madeira to Webb:

Now about the "Greek History". It goes on very slowly. I have to-day begun the fourth Book, from the Mahometan Conquest of Egypt, to the Recapture of Damietta by the Saracens—634–1223. I know you are afraid that I shall take an Oriental view, i.e. I suppose so Oriental that it will cease to be Catholick. I hope not. At the same time, without becoming a shade more Anglican, I do see more and

---

[1] Neale, *A History of the Holy Eastern Church: The Patriarchate of Alexandria*, vol. i, pp. vii ff.

[2] William Hodge Mill (1792–1853) was elected a Fellow of Trinity College, Cambridge, in 1814. He was the first principal of Bishop's College, Calcutta, 1820–1838. In the latter year he returned to England through ill health and became chaplain to Archbishop Howley. He supported Tractarian principles and the Cambridge Camden Society.

more clearly that the High Papal Theory is quite untenable. . . . I cannot make, as Montalembert does, visible union, or as the *British Critic* sometimes seemed to wish to do, the desire for visible union with the Chair of St Peter, the key-stone as it were, of the Church, at least not in the sense in which the Western Church has sometimes done. We *Orientals* take a more general view. The Rock on which the Church is built is St Peter, but it is a triple Rock, Antioch where he sat, Alexandria which he superintended, Rome where he suffered. You would be astonished at the weight of evidence in Doctors of the Western Church. By-the-bye, I must have you congratulate me on a Library turning up here. The Rector of the Seminary here has very kindly asked me to make any use I please of theirs, and it is a very good one, the edition of the Fathers particularly valuable. Is not this more than fortunate? My chief difficulty at present has been what view to take of the second Nicene Council. You must remember that neither in the East nor in the West had I anyone to whom I could look as a guide. . . .[1]

The following letter written a few weeks later gives some idea of the problems which arose in his mind as he set about his work:

I am much obliged to Dr Mill. Of course, during the periods where Alexandrian History is almost the same with that of the Catholick Church, such as in the Arian, Nestorian, and Monophysite controversies, I can only write popularly, but all after Mahomet will— I trust—be of a much higher character. I wish Dr Mill would give me his opinion as to the propriety of applying the term "Church" to any body having Apostolick Succession, 1. schismatical but not heretical, as the Donatists or Meletians; 2. heretical, but not schismatical, as the Aethiopian Jacobites and Nubians; 3. both heretical and schismatical, as the Aegyptian Jacobites.[2]

His researches made it necessary for him to write to various persons for information. The British chaplain at Alexandria answered inquiries from him. The British consul at Cairo waited on the Patriarch with questions sent to him. The Vicar of the Jacobite Patriarch of Alexandria provided much valuable information as to the state of that Communion.[3]

On 28 August 1844 Neale was able to write to Webb:

I will not repeat to you the success of my enquiries at Alexandria, and the compliments I have had from the Episcopos of the Catholic Convent of Alexandria. If you return by Geneva you may do me a great service. I am in correspondence with G. Diodati, Librarian of the "Library of the Republic", and he is to get for me copies of the

---

[1] *Letters*, p. 69.
[2] Ibid., pp. 72f.
[3] Neale, *History . . . Alexandria*, vol. i, p. xiv.

uncopied letters of poor Cyril Lucar which are kept there. If you could pay him what may be due, and bring the letters with you, I should be very glad. You might send him a line, fixing the time of your being there; and asking him to have the copies ready. This also: ask to see Cyril's Confession of Faith, I mean the original MS. If it is not forthcoming, hint that many, Romanists as well as Orientals, believe it to have been a Genevan forgery: and see what he says . . .[1]

Webb was of course abroad at the time. Cyril Lucar (1572–1638), whose life and career Neale relates at length, has been described as the first important theologian of the Eastern Church since the fall of Constantinople in 1453. A native of Crete, he studied in Italy. He later went to Alexandria, where he was ordained priest. He became Patriarch of Alexandria in 1602, and in 1620 Oecumenical Patriarch of Constantinople. He was very anti-Roman, and had much sympathy with the Calvinists. In 1629 he published his *Confessio*, which was a Calvinistic interpretation of the faith of the Eastern Orthodox Church. He had contacts with Archbishop Abbot of Canterbury. On account of his doctrinal position he made many enemies and was eventually murdered. Neale sums up "poor Cyril Lucar" as follows:

Considering what he did and what he suffered, the strength of his enemies, the weakness of his friends, the power of his early associations, the unkindness and unfairness of Rome, the bitterness of his persecutors, his own meekness, and patience, and great humility, and using towards him that charity of judgement which we ourselves should desire, we are justified in believing, that, notwithstanding his many errors,
After life's fitful fever, he sleeps well.[2]

The letters quoted above show how Neale collected together the material for his work on the Patriarchate of Alexandria. These two volumes, the first-fruits of his work on the Eastern Church, carried the following dedication:

To his holiness
ARTEMIUS
By Divine Mercy
Pope and Patriarch of Alexandria,
Libya, Pentapolis, and all the preaching of St Mark,
and Oecumenical Judge
This History of the Church of St Athanasius
is, with all humility,
inscribed.

[1] *Letters*, p. 74.   [2] Neale, *History . . . Alexandria*, vol. ii, p. 455.

9

It was Neale's original plan to write a history of all four Eastern Patriarchates in three separate portions, embracing respectively Alexandria, Antioch with Jerusalem, and Constantinople.[1] He had hoped that Webb would help him by accepting responsibility for two of the Patriarchates himself. But Webb, preoccupied with other matters, whilst willing to read proofs and to make suggestions, had neither the enthusiasm nor the aptitude for such a task. And so Neale was left to grapple with the undertaking himself.

His next publication on the subject was his two volumes entitled *History of the Holy Eastern Church—General Introduction*, published in 1850. In the preface he explains why these two volumes were necessary:

> While engaged on Alexandria, I found that it would be advisable, not to say necessary, to prefix a general Introduction regarding the rites, offices, faith, and customs of the Eastern Church. That Introduction it was designed to include in the first volume of the History of Alexandria; but, as I stated in the preface to that book, and as the present work proves, "it swelled to a size which precluded the possibility of such an arrangement." The History of Alexandria was therefore published by itself, and first; though the present Introduction was frequently referred to in the notes.[2]

He continues:

> This Introduction, then, in reality forms Part I of my History of the Eastern Church; Alexandria, which was published in 1847, is Part II; and if God spares me life and health, the history of Antioch and Jerusalem will be Part III; while Constantinople will, by itself, form Part IV.

The "General Introduction" is a very comprehensive and detailed account of matters relating to the Eastern Church. It consists of five books with the following titles:

1. The Geography of the Holy Eastern Church.
2. The Ecclesiology of the Holy Eastern Church.
3. The Liturgies of the Holy Eastern Church.
4. The Calendars and Office Books of the Holy Eastern Church.
5. Dissertation i. On Azymes (i.e. the question of the use of leavened or unleavened bread in the Eucharist).
   ii. On the Creed of the Armenian Church.

---

[1] Neale, *A History of the Holy Eastern Church: General Introduction*, vol. i, p. xi.
[2] Ibid.

iii. On the Procession of the Holy Ghost.

iv. On some points connected with the doctrine and discipline of the Holy Eastern Church: its position as regards Rome, and England: Conclusion.

The whole work in two volumes consisted of 1243 pages and took him six or seven years to complete. In the following year (1851) an Appendix containing lists of the sees was published.

In the introduction to Volume I Neale writes of the glory, mystery and indefinable nature of the Eastern Church. Always enthusiastic about new discoveries, he was greatly impressed, and felt that the Western Church had much to learn from her. The following passages give an insight into the impressions which he gained from his studies:

Theories of the Church, now principally drawn from the Annals of the Western Branch, might be corrected or confirmed by an enquiry into the wonders which the Eastern has been privileged to work, and the trials which she has been strengthened to endure. Details, which in the history of the Latin Communion seem isolated or anomalous, will fall into an intelligible system when confronted with the fortunes of the East. Roman developments will be tested by the unbroken traditions of sister communions; Roman arguments strengthened or disproved by a reference to Oriental facts. Uninterrupted successions of Metropolitans and Bishops stretch themselves to Apostolic times; venerable Liturgies exhibit doctrine unchanged, and discipline uncorrupted; the same Sacrifice is offered, the same hymns are chanted, by the Eastern Christians of today, as those which resounded in the churches of St Basil or St Firmilian. I shall write of Prelates not less faithful, of Martyrs not less constant, of Confessors not less generous, than those of Europe; shall shew every article of the Creed guarded with as much scrupulous jealousy; shall adduce a fresh crowd of witnesses to the Faith once for all delivered to the Saints. In the glow and splendour of Byzantine glory, in the tempests of the Oriental middle ages, in the desolation and tyranny of the Turkish Empire, the testimony of the same immutable Church remains unchanged. Extending herself from the sea of Okhotsk to the palaces of Venice, from the ice-fields that grind against the Solevetsky monastery to the burning jungles of Malabar, embracing a thousand languages, and nations, and tongues, but binding them together in the golden link of the same Faith, offering the Tremendous Sacrifice in a hundred Liturgies, but offering it to the same God, and with the same rites, fixing her Patriarchal Thrones in the same cities as when the Disciples were called Christians first at Antioch, and James, the brother of the Lord, finished his course at Jerusalem, oppressed by the devotees of the False Prophet, as once by the worshippers of false gods,—she is now, as she was from the beginning, multiplex in her arrangements, simple in her faith, difficult of comprehension to strangers, easily intelligible to her sons, widely scattered in her branches, hardly beset by her enemies, yet still and evermore, what she delights to call herself, One, Only, Holy, Catholic and Apostolic.[1]

Then he goes on to refer to the adverse criticism which has been directed against this part of the Church. She has not escaped, any more than her Great Head, the tongue of calumny. Protestant controversialists, Roman theologians, infidel travellers, all have attacked her.

For eighteen hundred years, it might be answered, this venerable Communion has fought the good fight, and borne about in her body the marks of the Lord Jesus. Since she armed Athanasius against Arius, and sent forth Cyril against Nestorius, unnumbered heresies have assailed her; foes in every shape have surrounded her; without have been fightings, within fears; her existence itself has oftentimes been a very agony; yet the gates of hell have never prevailed against her. Idolatry and apostasy have attempted her subjugation, and confessed her invincible; Kings and Caliphs, Emperors and Sultans, have stood up against her, but the King of kings and Lord of lords has been on her side.[2]

In spite of numerous attacks on all sides the Eastern Church had survived, and Neale had great hopes for her future:

But the Eastern Church survived: dispirited, persecuted, humbled to the very dust, from generation to generation she handed down the power of the Keys, and offered the Mystic Sacrifice; and even when most depressed by the scholastic subtleties and political intrigues of her Roman Sister, even then she triumphed most gloriously over Calvinism and its attendant heresies. And at this time, when everything betokens the approaching dissolution of the Ottoman Empire, when the most widely extended nation, and the mightiest Emperor in the world, profess the Oriental Faith, when the great line of railway which will connect England with India, the main artery of universal commerce, must intersect in half its length the domain of the Eastern Church, it is impossible, humanly speaking, but that a bright future is still before her.[3]

In this same introduction Neale relates some of the difficulties which confront the historian of the Eastern Church. First of all, writers of the Roman Communion did not interest themselves much in the annals of a body which they regarded as schismatical, and so the historian had to rely mainly on Eastern sources.

[1] Ibid., pp. 1ff.   [2] Ibid.   [3] Ibid., p. 5.

Secondly, a general history of the Eastern Church as a whole by Oriental writers did not exist:

> Each of the Patriarchates has, more or less satisfactorily, its own series of chronologers, for we can dignify them by no higher title. But their action and re-action on each other, their existence as a whole, their inward life, the working of the One Spirit in every member, these things are dismissed as unimportant, or omitted as unknown. Hence the annals of the Eastern Patriarchates are the mere skeletons of history. These bones must be collected and clothed with flesh and sinews, and (if it may be) endued with the breath of life . . .[1]

Thirdly, the Eastern historians had no common language. Greek, in various degrees of corruption, Arabic, Syriac, Russian, and Armenian were the principal sources from which materials had to be obtained. Besides these difficulties he refers to:

> the great difficulty of arriving at the fountain-head of information: the precious MSS mouldering in far distant monasteries . . . the destruction of ancient documents, the unexplained and inexplicable contradictions which the carelessness of Eastern writers has introduced: the tedious prolixity in which they involve their facts; the total absence of true criticism which they manifest; the unfortunate pertinacity with which they relate at the greatest length those matters of which they themselves had least personal know- ledge; the want of any faithful clue to the labyrinth of doubts and hesitations in which the historian of the Oriental Church is involved; these things might well suffice to deter the warmest lover of Ecclesiastical History from attempting,—whatever be its interest,— that of the East.[2]

Neale himself, however, was by no means deterred by such difficulties. To discover, sort out, and record the intricate history of the Eastern Church was a task which fascinated and delighted him. As we have seen, most men would have shrunk from such a gigantic and complicated labour, but to him the seemingly impossible was only a challenge to put to the proof his favourite maxim: "If it is possible, it *shall* be done; and if it is impossible it *must* be done."[3]

In writing this history Neale expressed his desire to identify himself as far as possible with the Eastern Church: "I have at least endeavoured, so far as might be, to put myself in an

---

[1] Ibid., p. 6.   [2] Ibid., pp. 6, 7.   [3] *Memoir*, p. 295.

Oriental position, and from that position to review the scenes which pass before us."[1]

He dedicated this two-volume *Introduction* to His Imperial Majesty Nicolai I, Emperor and Autocrat of all the Russias. This was acknowledged by the Emperor, and Neale received a grant of £100 from him for his work. On 10 June 1851 the Reverend Eugene Popoff, chaplain to the Russian Embassy in London, wrote to Neale:

> His Excellency our Ambassador, Baron de Brunmow, has kindly charged me to announce to you, that His Majesty, the Emperor of Russia, in acknowledgment of the value of your arduous and useful work on "the History of the Holy Eastern Church", as well as an encouragement in its continuance, has been graciously pleased to grant you the sum of £100.[2]

At about the same time he received from Philaret, Metropolitan of Moscow, some icons, which he afterwards always kept in his study, together with a Slavonic Service Book inscribed with the words: "God's blessing be on all those who study the ancient Liturgies and rites of the Church in preparation for the future union of the Churches.—Ph. M. Moscow."[3]

Such recognition of his work was a source of great happiness to Neale, and was in some ways a compensation for the persecution and neglect which he found in his own Church.

As we have seen, Neale lived to complete only Parts I and II of his *History of the Holy Eastern Church,* i.e. the *General Introduction* and *The Patriarchate of Alexandria*. He did, however, leave some very full notes for the Patriarchate of Antioch. These notes were later edited by the Reverend George Williams and published in 1873. The latter pays the following tribute to Neale's work on the Eastern Church:

> The most striking features to those who had known the author as a writer of life-like fiction, and the uncompromising champion of distinctive Catholic teaching, were, first, the complete subordination of his exuberant poetical imagination to the strict requirements of historical accuracy; and then the rigid impartiality of his estimate of moral worth, unbiassed by theological prejudices and pre-dilections.[4]

---

[1] *History . . . General Introduction,* vol. i, p. 8.
[2] Towle, *Memoir,* p. 175.
[3] *Memoir,* p. 9b.
[4] *A History of the Holy Eastern Church: The Patriarchate of Antioch,* pp. x, xi.

In addition to his volumes on the history of the Eastern Church, Neale published in 1859 *Greek Liturgies of SS. Mark, James, Clement, Chrysostom, and Basil*. In the same year he produced English translations of these liturgies, including that of the Church of Malabar, under the title *Translations of the Primitive Liturgies*. In the preface to the latter he wrote:

> It has for many years been my desire to render these most pure sources of Eucharistical Doctrine accessible to all my brethren. Hitherto the whole of them have not been procurable in Greek, except with difficulty, and at a heavy expense: in English not at all.[1]

Thus Neale made the chief Eastern liturgies accessible to the English-speaking world.

In 1859 he also published another book concerned with the Eastern Church entitled, *Voices from the East*, with the sub-title, *Documents on the present state and working of the Oriental Church translated from the original Russ, Slavonic, and French, with Notes*. In the preface Neale writes:

> While slowly and laboriously carrying on my "History of the Holy Eastern Church", I cannot but feel the deepest interest in the present prospects, and hopes, and trials, and efforts, of that most venerable communion. The documents which appear in the present volume are such as are calculated to give the latest information on the state of the Oriental Church; and they have the advantage of allowing its members to speak for themselves.[2]

This collection of essays and letters, mostly by Russian writers, bear such titles as "Catholic Orthodoxy and Roman Catholicism"; "The Dogma of the Immaculate Conception from an Orthodox Point of View"; and "The Expositions of Faith employed by the Holy Eastern Church."

One of the disputed points of doctrine between the Eastern and the Western Church is the *Filioque* clause in the Nicene Creed. The words "and the Son" were added to "Who proceedeth from the Father" in the Western Church. It is interesting to know that Neale held the view that the Eastern Church was right and the Western Church was wrong in this matter. In his *History of the Holy Eastern Church—General Introduction* he devotes Dissertation iii to this subject. He concludes with the following words:

[1] Neale, *Translations of the Primitive Liturgies* (2nd edn, 1869), p. vii.
[2] *Voices from the East* (1859), p. v.

English Churchmen will hardly deny that, let the dogma of the double Procession be never so true, its insertion in the inviolable Creed was an act utterly unjustifiable, and throws on the Roman Church the chief guilt in the horrible schism of 1054. It was done in the teeth of the veto passed in the sixth session of the Council of Ephesus, in the fifth of Chalcedon, in the sixth collation of the second of Constantinople, and in the seventeenth of the third of Constantinople. It was done against the express command of a most holy Pope, himself a believer in the double Procession, who is now with God. No true union—experience has shewn it—can take place between the Churches, till the *Filioque* be omitted from the Creed, even if a truly Oecumenical Synod should afterwards proclaim the truth of the doctrine. And I end therefore, as I commenced, with the words of our great Bishop Pearson: "Thus began the schism; never thenceforth to be reconciled, till the word *Filioque* be omitted from the Creed."[1]

In a letter to Webb on 30 January 1851 Neale wrote as follows:

I suppose that Blackmore, Palmer and I are the only men in the English Church who are thoroughly convinced that the Latin doctrine is grievously erroneous, suspected of heresy, and even (if logically carried out) heretical.[2]

Yet twenty-five years later Dr Pusey told Dr Liddon that "if the English Church gave up the *Filioque*, he must either shut his eyes and go to Rome, or trust that God would save him out of any Church at all. He could have no part in it."[3] Pusey, in spite of his great learning, had little contact with the Eastern Church, and did not understand her position.[4] Neale was far ahead of him in this matter.

There is one other aspect of Neale's work in connection with the Eastern Church to which reference must be made. In the preface to his *History of the Holy Eastern Church—General Introduction*, Neale refers to the difficulty of obtaining information from the Orthodox authorities at Constantinople. He describes this lack of co-operation as "doubtless one example among many of the jealousy excited against the English Church, by the miserable proceedings of her so called representative at Jerusalem".[5] He is here referring to Bishop Gobat, the Anglican Bishop in

---

[1] *History . . . General Introduction*, vol. ii, p. 1168.
[2] *Letters*, p. 162; see also p. 131.
[3] J. O. Johnston, *Life and Letters of H. P. Liddon* (1904), p. 189.
[4] C. B. Moss, *The Old Catholic Movement, Its Origin and History* (1948), p. 269.
[5] *History . . . General Introduction*, vol. i, p. xiv.

Jerusalem, and his proselytizing efforts amongst Orthodox Christians. An outline of the story of the Anglo-Prussian Bishopric in Jerusalem is given by the late Canon S. L. Ollard.[1] The founding of this bishopric was one of the factors which led to Newman's secession. Gobat, the second of the bishops in the scheme, was consecrated in 1846. It was in 1851 that he was accused of proselytizing. This action was contrary to the declaration of the Archbishop of Canterbury at the time of the inauguration of the scheme. Neale and others took up the matter with indignation. The copy of a Protest signed by over a thousand English clergymen was sent in Greek to the Eastern Patriarchs. Neale had no small part in drawing up the Protest and collecting the signatures.[2]

The only Eastern Orthodox countries which Neale was able to visit were Dalmatia and Montenegro. He made a tour of the Eastern Adriatic countries in the summer of 1860. At Montenegro he found it so curious "to see an intensely Catholic population, yet spitting at the Latin, and having as the usual name from [sic] Roman Catholics, *men of the dog's faith*".[3]

He always hoped one day to visit Russia, and he received several invitations from friends and acquaintances in that country, but he was never able to make the journey. Through his history of the Eastern Church, however, he was well known to the Church authorities there. As we have seen, he received presents from the Emperor, and from the Metropolitan of Moscow, as well as from other leading members of the Russian Church. On 26 February 1860 he wrote to Webb:

> I wish you could see my glorious *Icons*. . . . The Archimandrite sent a very pretty Madonna to our Mother [i.e. Superior of the Convent]. I had no idea till now lately how big a man I was in Russia. I have the censures of the Central Committee on my "Introduction" previous to its translation. They are very amusing.[4]

He then goes to say that a Russian translation of one of his stories, *The Lily of Tiflis*, "has been a perfect *hit*".

Neale's close association with members of the Eastern Church is shown by the fact that the Archimandrite Stratuli and the Reverend Eugene Popoff, chaplain of the Russian embassy in London, were present at the laying of the foundation stone of

[1] *Dictionary of English Church History* (1948), p. 308.
[2] *Memoir*, p. 212b. *Letters*, p. 221.
[3] *Letters*, p. 326.
[4] Ibid., p. 311.

127

the present St Margaret's Convent on St Margaret's Day 1865. The Archimandrite gave the blessing. Neale was in touch with Popoff for nearly twenty years, and derived great help from him in arriving at an understanding of Eastern Orthodoxy. The following interesting facts are related about Neale's death and funeral:

> Another circumstance witnessed to his widespread influence, and that was that around the same grave were representatives of all branches of the Church Catholic, Greek, Roman, and Anglican. When, too, the tidings of his death were telegraphed to the Patriarch of Holy Russia, the same bell tolled for Dr Neale, which is used for dignified ecclesiastics of the Orthodox Communion.[1]

Writing of Neale's *History of the Holy Eastern Church* Dr Dugmore says that he "opened new windows for those who had hitherto been concerned solely with the history and liturgy of Western Christendom".[2] More than any other churchman of his own day Neale made a move to break down the insularity of the Church of England, and to persuade her members to look beyond her own borders. As with his Eastern hymns, so with his writings on the Eastern Church,[3] he brought to the attention of members of the Church of England a great part of Catholic Christendom, about which the majority were almost entirely ignorant. As a result of his work, Eastern Orthodoxy was henceforth something with which to be reckoned in any consideration of reunion in the Church of England. By his indefatigable labours on the history of the Eastern Church Neale undoubtedly won a great respect for the Church of England from leading Orthodox churchmen, especially from those in Russia. His work has clearly been an important factor in the better understanding between Anglicanism and Eastern Orthodoxy which has been reached during the past hundred years. To-day he would no doubt regret that, a century after his work, a closer rapprochement has not yet been reached between the two Communions, but he would be profoundly thankful that the work, which he largely initiated, is still going on.

[1] George Huntington, *Random Recollections* (1896), p. 222.
[2] C. W. Dugmore, *Ecclesiastical History No Soft Option* (1959), p. 15.
[3] These writings included historical novels. The best is *Theodora Phranza, or the Fall of Constantinople* (1857).

I I

The Church of Holland

NEALE had an extraordinary gift for opening up vistas of Church history which had been forgotten, and for bringing to the light parts of the Catholic Church about which the majority of English churchpeople were entirely ignorant. In the previous chapter we saw how, after many years of neglect, he again made people in this country think about the great Church of the East. In the middle of the nineteenth century hardly anybody in England had heard of the ancient Catholic Church in Holland, founded in the seventh century by the Englishman, Willibrord, and in spite of the Reformation and Counter-Reformation still preserving its catholicity and independence of Rome. It was Neale who brought this Church to the notice of churchmen in this country, and in effect started a movement which was to culminate in full intercommunion between the Church of England and the Old Catholic Communion on the continent of Europe in 1932.

Neale was a great traveller. While he was at Sackville College, he spent most of his holidays visiting different countries in Europe, studying the ecclesiology and the general state of the Church. In the summer of 1851 he visited Holland, and made his first acquaintance with the Church of Utrecht and the Archbishop at that time, Johannes van Santen.[1] His second visit to Holland was in 1854. On 9 October he wrote to Webb from Utrecht:

I got here from Antwerp on Thursday evening, and have received every kindness from the Archbishop. . . . Sunday I went to Mass at St Gertrude's. It is a very curious Office. One forgets that 150 years of separation must give a different air and manner to the same ritual—especially as I doubt whether any of the set have ever been

---

[1] Towle, *Memoir*, p. 219.

into a Roman Catholic Church (for they scarcely go out of Holland).
I cannot give you a better idea of it than by saying that it struck me
as the same thing that it would be if a set of Puseyites went through
Mass—a great deal of stiffness or awkwardness, and slowness. It is,
as you know, a modern Church, gilt and white—that sort of thing—
narrow, high galleries; centre, chairs for women; side, benches for
men; almost everyone had books, and the children fidgetted with
them just as they do in England. According to a Canon of their
Council of 1763, there was no music during Consecration. The
Archbishop celebrated—it was a Mass that I could neither call
High nor Low; he had no deacon nor sub-deacon, but there was
music etc., and everything else as in High Mass. There was only a
Crucifix and pix, besides candles on the Altar; very few images
anywhere—and those of plaster. The Archbishop's *submissa voce* was
so loud that I could hear every word of the Consecration. On the
whole, I was not pleased with that Office. When it was over,
Mulder came in, and, after reading the Epistle and Gospel in Dutch
from the pulpit, preached. I then had a talk with the Archbishop,
and then with Mulder. They have quite loaded me with books. . . .[1]

From the time of his first visit to Holland, Neale wished to
give to his fellow-countrymen the opportunity of becoming
better acquainted with the history of this Church. His study of
the Church over a period of about seven years resulted in his
book, *A History of the So-called Jansenist Church of Holland*, published in 1858. As with his history of the Eastern Church, he
took great pains to give as accurate an account as possible of the
history of this Church, examining many of the original documents
at Utrecht.

At the beginning of his study he sums up the position of this
Church in relation to the rest of Western Christendom:

Engaged for a century and a half in a struggle of almost unparalleled
inequality, where ecclesiastical power, wealth, *prestige*, and numbers
a thousand times told, were on the one side, and simply justice and
right on the other, she has come down to our times, persecuted,
but not forsaken, cast down, but not destroyed. A taunt and a
byeword to the rampant Ultramontanism of modern Europe, she
has calmly and trustfully held her own, proclaimed her unshaken
attachment to Catholic union and the Catholic faith, appealed,
from time to time, against the unjust sentences extorted from the
court of Rome, and awaits, in patience and hope, those brighter
days when her appeal can be heard, when her isolation shall be
removed, and her separate history again merged in the general
annals of the Western Church.

[1] *Letters*, pp. 228f.

He considers that the history of this Church should be of special interest to those members of the Church of England "who lament our isolation from the rest of Christendom, by setting before them a memorable example of patience and perseverance, through evil report and good report, on the part of another, and equally separated, national communion".[1]

We shall now give an outline of Neale's account of this Church. The Church of Utrecht owed its origin to missionary work from England. In the seventh century Willibrord, a native of Northumbria, who had been educated by the monks of Ripon and had later gone to the Irish Abbey of Rathmelsigi, was sent to Frisia to preach the Gospel. A few years later in 695 he was consecrated by Pope Sergius as Archbishop of the Frisians. Pepin, the Frankish king, granted him Utrecht for his episcopal see. For nearly fifty years Willibrord laboured in Frisia, and brought multitudes into the fold of the Church. At the time of his death his friend Boniface (Winfrid of Crediton), who had done so much for building up the Church in Germany, and who then was Archbishop of Mainz, decided to spend the last days of his life in pioneer missionary work in Frisia. He made his way to that country, but in less than a year after his arrival in 754 or 755 he suffered martyrdom at Dokkum.

After the death of Boniface the claim of the see of Cologne to jurisdiction over Utrecht was recognized by the Pope, and the see of Utrecht became part of the province of Cologne until 1559. According to Neale the first twenty prelates were mostly worthy successors of Willibrord, and several were to be reckoned among the saints. They ended however with St Bernulphus, who died in 1054. After him came the times of degeneracy. The bishops became temporal lords and warriors rather than prelates. The duties of their pastoral office were exercised by suffragans, while they themselves headed armies.[2] The bishopric of Utrecht grew in worldly wealth and power. Seven provinces, including such towns as Amsterdam, Haarlem, Leyden, and Rotterdam, and a considerable part of modern Belgium, came under the authority of the bishop.[3]

Up to the twelfth century the bishops of Utrecht had been

---

[1] Neale, *A History of the So-called Jansenist Church of Holland* (1858), p. 61.
[2] Ibid., p. 63.
[3] Ibid., p. 65.

elected popularly by clergy and laity. In 1145 Pope Eugenius III, at the petition of the Emperor Conrad III, restricted the election to the two chapters of the Cathedral and St Saviour's. Afterwards the right of election was extended to three other churches, which thenceforward constituted the chapter of Utrecht. Neale points out that whereas the new régime gave occasion to fiercer quarrels and more deadly outbreaks than the old, the change was of the highest importance and affected the very existence of the Church of Holland.[1] In later times, when resisting the Pope, the Church could always claim the right of the chapter to elect its own bishop.

In the sixteenth century another factor arose which was to strengthen the Church in her later struggle with the Pope. Philip of Burgundy, the fifty-seventh bishop, obtained a brief from Leo X conceding that "neither he, nor any of his successors, nor any of their clergy or laity, should ever, in the first instance, have his cause evoked to any external tribunal, not even under pretence of any apostolic letters whatever; and that all such proceedings would be *ipso facto* null and void". Neale then states: "The Pontiff was here only confirming an inalienable right of the Church; but his confirmation was providential, as viewed in respect to the great schism that was, in the course of years, to break out."[2] The succeeding bishop, Henry of Bavaria, having been driven from the city by a faction, surrendered his temporal sovereignty to the Emperor Charles V, on condition that the Emperor restored him to his see. Neale comments: "Thus the Church of Utrecht lost her temporal lordship; and, perjured as the bishop was who ceded it, can we doubt that she was well rid of so burdensome an appendage?"[3]

In spite of the worldliness in high places in the fourteenth and fifteenth centuries, this Church produced such outstanding spiritual leaders as John de Ruysbroek (or Jan van Ruysbroeck, 1293–1381), Geert Groote (or Gerardus Magnus, 1340–84), founder of "The Brothers of the Common Life", and Thomas à Kempis (1380–1471). "The Brothers of the Common Life" were not a monastic order. The members did not take vows, but they were united by a voluntary association. They laid stress on teaching and founded schools. "The order, then, was designed to teach the young, to send out preachers, and to recommend the study of Holy Scripture; in short it was a true and holy reform, and was therefore certain to find bitter opposition. Deventer was the centre of the movement."[1] Geert Groote was a zealous preacher, and Neale compares him to John Wesley.

In his account of Thomas à Kempis, Neale says that it is now almost a settled point among ecclesiastical scholars that Thomas was not the author of the *Imitation of Christ*, and he gives six reasons to support this view. He concludes: "After all, a far more edifying point of consideration than that of its authorship, is the comfort and blessing which, for nearly four hundred years, the 'Imitation' has been to every Christian nation."[2]

Neale then refers to the scholarship of the later brothers:

> With the death of Thomas, the learned generation may be said to have commenced. Overyssel and Guelderland were undoubtedly, at the epoch of the invention of printing, the most learned countries in Europe; and the first leading colleges were at Deventer, Zutphen, Zwolle, and Kampen. The Cardinal Cusa and Pope Hadrian VI owed their erudition to these institutions; and in 1476 a young lad named Gerard was received at Deventer, who afterwards became known to all the literary world as Desiderius Erasmus. From these, as from a centre, radiated schools into every part of north-western Europe.[3]

As time went on "The Brothers of the Common Life" developed into six different "families"—the Belgian, the German, the Italian, the Portuguese, the Sicilian, and the Genoese. Of the German "family" Luther said in 1534: "Would that all monasteries would teach and hold the Word of God as earnestly as this."[4] The Dutch Brothers were eventually absorbed by the House of Canons Regular at Windesheim. But the whirlwind of the Reformation swept the congregation out of Holland, and "it had not the vitality to propagate itself in the neighbouring countries".[5]

In the sixteenth century Philip II of Spain, who succeeded to the hereditary possessions of his father Charles V, persuaded the Pope to increase the number of bishops in the Netherlands and to set up a number of new provinces and dioceses. Utrecht was thus again made an archbishopric with the five new sees of Haarlem, Deventer, Groningen, Leeuwarden, and Middleburg. One object of Philip in setting up the new bishoprics was to have

[1] Ibid., pp. 78f.   [4] Ibid., pp. 100f.
[2] Ibid., p. 99.   [5] Ibid., p. 102.
[3] Ibid.

a better organization for suppressing heresy.[1] The Spanish Inquisition was introduced in 1565. The Dutch War of Independence followed soon after (1568–1648). According to Neale this was "characterized by cruelty on both sides scarcely elsewhere to be found in the annals of the human race". He adds: "It is probable that the palm of barbarity—it is certain that of duplicity —must be awarded to the Protestants."[2] The outcome of the war was that the seven northern provinces—Holland, Zealand, Utrecht, Gelderland, Overyssel, Friesland, and Groningen— became a Republic. The new Republic adopted the Reformed religion.

In 1560 Frederick Schenk had been consecrated as the first Archbishop of Utrecht since St Willibrord. Five years later in 1565 he held a provincial synod, which accepted the decrees of the Council of Trent, but the chapters protested against any interference with their capitular rights.[3]

In 1580 through the influence of extremists the practice of the Roman Catholic religion was forbidden by the magistrates of Utrecht. In spite of this decree a large proportion of the people remained Roman Catholic, and worship was carried on secretly. In the same year Archbishop Schenk died, and the see remained vacant until 1602. It so happened that at this time for various reasons the other five sees of the new province also fell vacant.

In 1592 Sasbold Vosmeer, Dean of St Mary's Church, The Hague, was appointed by the Pope to be Vicar Apostolic of the United Provinces, but he never ceased to urge the re-establishment of the see of Utrecht. In the same year the Jesuits first entered the country. It was their arrival and subsequent policy which finally led to the breach between the Church of Utrecht and the Roman Church. The Jesuits' idea of the Church left no room for local or diocesan rights. They wished themselves to control the Roman Catholic Church in the Netherlands. For this reason they continually persuaded the Pope not to recognize the Archbishop of Utrecht but to rule by vicars apostolic.

In 1602 Vosmeer decided to go to Rome to plead his cause against the Jesuits. "While meditating this journey he was seized with an illness, which bore every appearance of poison.

[1] C. B. Moss, *The Old Catholic Movement, Its Origins and History* (1948), pp. 92ff.
[2] *History . . . Church of Holland*, pp. 109f. Cf. Moss, op. cit., p. 94.
[3] *History . . . Church of Holland*, pp. 108f.

He himself constantly attributed it to his opponents."[1] When he at last reached Rome, Pope Clement VIII received him with courtesy, and proposed that he should himself accept the archbishopric of Utrecht. Vosmeer, however, urged the appointment of a younger man. In the end, much against his will, having been elected by the chapter, he was consecrated with the title of Archbishop of Philippi. This title was chosen ostensibly in order not to offend the Dutch Government. It was understood, however, that he should assume his genuine title of Archbishop of Utrecht, as soon as better times came. At the same time the Jesuits tried to show that Vosmeer was merely a vicar apostolic with a title *in partibus*.[2] Neale proves that this was quite untrue.

Six weeks after his consecration Vosmeer was accused of high treason by the Dutch Government and banished from Holland. He retired to Cologne, from where he ruled his diocese, and visited it only at the risk of his life. He was constantly harassed by the Jesuits, and wrote to his brother: "The inconvenience caused by the Protestants is less than the affliction originated by the Jesuits."[3]

Vosmeer died in 1614. Philip Rovenius was elected as his successor, but for various reasons was not consecrated until 1620. Unlike his predecessor, Rovenius managed to live for a time at Utrecht. Like his predecessor, he had to struggle against the intrigues of the Jesuits, and he had to go to Rome in order to have his rights confirmed.[4]

The last Archbishop of Utrecht to die in full communion with Rome was Johannes van Neercassel (1661–86). He also suffered from the attacks of the Jesuits and had to go to Rome to defend himself. Here his case met with some success, but many ridiculed him because of his simple way of life.

At this time some of the French Jansenists, who had been harried out of France by the Jesuits, took refuge in Holland. The Jansenists took their name from Cornelius Jansen (1585–1638), who was a professor at the University of Louvain until be became Bishop of Ypres in 1636. In 1640 his *Augustinus* was published. This book gave the teaching of St Augustine on grace, and was an attack on the Jesuits. It started a movement which aimed at reforming the Roman Catholic Church from within. Its centre

[1] Ibid., p. 120.   [3] Ibid., p. 124.
[2] Ibid., p. 121.   [4] Moss, op. cit., p. 100.

was at Port-Royal. The Jansenists became strong supporters of the Church of Utrecht against the Jesuits. Notable amongst them was Van Espen (1646–1728) the great canonist, who died at Amersfoort in communion with the Church of Utrecht.[1]

The archbishop who was to succeed Neercassel was Peter Codde. He was accused by the Jesuits of being a Jansenist and a Gallican. Through their intrigues Theodore de Cock was appointed Pro-Vicar Apostolic of the United Provinces, and Codde was deposed. The chapters of Utrecht and Haarlem, however, decided not to recognize the authority of de Cock.[2] This was the beginning of the schism between the two parties in the Dutch Roman Catholic Church. From that time the Church of Utrecht had to fight for its freedom and its life. The Jesuits did all they could to fill the parishes with ultramontane priests. Congregations were taught that it was worse to attend a Jansenist service than a Protestant one. But the chapter of Utrecht firmly held on to its constitutional rights, and it was invariably supported by the canonists of the University of Louvain.

There came a time, however, in the eighteenth century when the Church of Utrecht had no bishops. Peter Codde died in 1710. Pope Innocent XIII ignored the appeal of the chapter to be allowed to elect, and to have an archbishop consecrated for the see. The opinion of Van Espen and other canonists was sought. Their judgement was that in special circumstances the chapter had the right to elect their archbishop, and to have him consecrated, without the consent of the Pope, and that in case of necessity one bishop alone might consecrate.[3]

The chapter proceeded to act on this judgement. Cornelius Steenoven was elected, and on 15 October 1724 was consecrated by the Bishop of Babylon (Dominique Marie Varlet—a French Missionary bishop, who through the machinations of the Jesuits had been unable to occupy his see) in his private chapel at Amsterdam.[4]

In the following year Benedict XIII, newly elected to the papal throne, declared the consecration illicit and execrable. The clergy of Utrecht, however, were not to be intimidated. They pointed out the errors which the Pope's brief contained.[5] But after a

---

[1] *History . . . Church of Holland*, p. 274.
[2] Moss, op. cit., pp. 106f.
[3] *History . . . Church of Holland*, p. 249.
[4] Ibid., p. 256.
[5] Ibid., pp. 258f.

month the archbishop was seized with a serious illness and died a few days later, having professed his belief in the Catholic faith and the prerogatives of the Roman See, and having appealed for himself and his Church to an Oecumenical Council.[1] The Church of Utrecht was again without a bishop.

A month after the death of Steenoven, Cornelius John Barchman Wuytiers was elected by the chapter of Utrecht to fill the vacant see. The same procedure was followed as in the case of Steenoven. Wuytiers was consecrated by the Bishop of Babylon in the church of St James at the Hague on 30 September 1725.

According to Neale one of the most remarkable events of the episcopate of Wuytiers was the attempt made by him to bring about the union of the Eastern and Western Churches. He was also responsible for setting up a seminary at Amersfoort.

Wuytiers died suddenly in 1731, and was succeeded by Theodore van der Croon, also consecrated by the Bishop of Babylon.

The next archbishop was Peter John Meindaerts, who was elected in 1739. He was the last to be consecrated by the Bishop of Babylon. The fulminations of the new Pope, Benedict XIV, against this act were particularly strong. In his brief the archbishop is characterized as "a child of iniquity, a most unnatural son of the tenderest of fathers, a deceitful and savage wolf, an accomplished seducer, a madman, whose case is almost desperate".[2]

In 1742 the Bishop of Babylon died, and in the same year Archbishop Meindaerts provided for the succession by consecrating a bishop for the see of Haarlem, which had been vacant since 1587. Sixteen years later, in 1758, Bartholomew John Byefield, one of the canons of Utrecht, was consecrated as titular Bishop of Deventer. Thus the Church of Holland came to have its three bishops. These three sees have continued to modern times.

In 1763 Archbishop Meindaerts held a provincial synod. Its main purpose was to condemn the teaching of Peter Le Clerc, a French subdeacon living at Amsterdam. He "had asserted doctrines utterly opposed to Catholic tradition asserting the equality of bishops and priests, and denying the divine right of the former, and other matters of equal moment. It was thought that now was the time for the Church of Utrecht to prove her attachment to Western unity; and that, while Le Clerc's errors were condemned,

[1] Ibid., pp. 259f.   [2] Ibid., p. 283.

a censure might be passed on the corrupted morals of the Jesuits."[1]

Briefly, the synod preserved the rights of the separated clergy if they acknowledged the authority of their own bishops. It decided to hold a triennial council in accordance with the injunctions of the Council of Trent. It stated that it recites the Nicene Creed as that in use through the "One Holy Roman Catholic and Apostolic Church". It anathematized all errors and heresies anathematized by the Council of Trent, and accepted Bossuet's *Exposition de la Foi*. In addition the errors both of Le Clerc and of the Jesuit corrupters of morality were denounced.[2] In condemning Le Clerc's account of the schism between Rome and Constantinople, and accusing the Greek Christians of being schismatics, Neale points out that the synod was really cutting the ground away under its own feet: "It must be clear that if *Utrecht* were substituted for Greece . . . the condemnation pronounced must be equally just."[3]

According to Neale the acts of the synod were received "with general applause". "From many bishops in France, Italy, Spain, and Germany, letters of congratulation and communion were received."[4] The Jesuits, however, succeeded in having the synod condemned by a papal bull.[5]

The downfall of the Jesuits, whom Neale calls "the great enemies of Utrecht",[6] came with the suppression of the Society by Pope Clement XIV in 1773. This suppression might have brought some peace to the Church of Utrecht. But the next Pope, Pius VI, had no sympathy with the Dutch Church. During his pontificate the French Revolution took place, and men's thoughts were turned in another direction.

The French Revolution, followed by the rise of Napoleon and his Concordat with the Pope in 1801, did not much help the hardpressed Church of Holland. She could no longer look for any support from the former Gallican party in France.

In 1810 Holland was annexed to the French Empire.[7] The Archbishop of Utrecht, Jacob van Rhijn, had died suddenly in 1808: Neale suggests that he was probably poisoned.[8] The chapter had been forbidden by the Government to elect a

[1] Ibid., pp. 294f.
[2] Ibid., pp. 298ff.
[3] Ibid., p. 302.
[4] Ibid., p. 323.
[5] Ibid., pp. 326f.
[6] Ibid., p. 330.
[7] Ibid., p. 346.
[8] Ibid., p. 344.

successor. In January 1810 the Bishop of Haarlem died. Thus once again the existence of the Church of Holland depended on one life, that of Bishop de Jong of Deventer.

In 1811 Napoleon came to Utrecht. The Emperor remained firm in his refusal to permit any election of an archbishop. "I will myself treat with the Pope and arrange the organization of the Church of Holland", he said. In the meanwhile the Church was to experience its narrowest escape. "On a dark winter's night, Bishop de Jong, returning home along the edge of a dyke, missed his footing, and fell into the canal. For some minutes his life was in imminent danger: on that life hung the fortunes of the Church of Utrecht."[1]

The French were driven from the Netherlands in 1814. As soon as possible the chapter of Utrecht proceeded to fill the archiepiscopal see. Willibrord van Os was elected, and consecrated by the Bishop of Deventer. Five years later Johannes Bon was consecrated Bishop of Haarlem, and so the three sees were once again filled.

Neale relates the following "remarkable circumstance" about this particular bishop:

Bishop Bon was the only prelate who escaped excommunication from Rome. This was owing to the good offices of Cardinal Gonzalvi, then Secretary of State. Eight years later he was nominated by the King of Holland to the vacant bishopric of Bruges. A curious ecclesiastical question was now raised. Would Rome grant the Bulls of a Jansenist Bishop? Would the old discussion about a succession derived from one prelate alone be revived? No difficulty of the latter kind was experienced; and in the Consistory of Cardinals the punning remark was made, *Dominus Bonus non potest esse pastor malus*. But, from other causes the scheme fell to the ground.[2]

Neale makes the following comments on the state of the Church of Holland at that time:

The marvellous events of the preceding thirty years, the general confusion of Europe, the rise and fall of empires, the general march of ecclesiastical events, had thrown the little Church of Holland into the shade. She had been, as it were, forgotten. A century before, the eyes of all Europe were upon her; now her existence was known but to few. The perfect liberty given to Catholics, in common with all sectarian bodies, opened a wide door to Rome; and one of the most practical arguments of the National Church was cut away from

<hr>

[1] Ibid., p. 347.   [2] Ibid., pp. 349f.

her by the appointment of Vicars-Apostolic. While not to belong to the Church of Utrecht was to be cut off from episcopacy, and, in particular, to be left without the possibility of receiving the grace of Confirmation, there was a tangible argument to every religious mind—however little able to fathom the theory of separation—in favour of Utrecht. Again, at the commencement of the schism, the numbers were three to two on the side of the National Church. Now, on awaking to the new era of readjusted Europe, the communion of Utrecht contained 5000 souls; that of Rome in Holland, about one million. Yet the little band of "Ancient Roman Catholics" suffered no defection; it has, if anything, increased its numbers since the recovered independence of Holland.[1]

Johannes van Santen, with whom Neale was acquainted, was elected and consecrated archbishop in 1825. As in the case of all his predecessors the chapter applied to the Pope for confirmation, but as usual received no answer. After the consecration had taken place the usual brief of excommunication was received.[2]

A month later the archbishop and his two suffragans addressed "an admirable encyclic" to all bishops of the Catholic Church. Neale sums it up as follows:

It goes over the old ground calmly and briefly, states the facts of the schism; proves the nullity and invalidity of the pretended excommunication of the Court of Rome; shows that there is no charge of heresy . . . protests against the appellation of Jansenist, and invokes the mediation of the united episcopate with the Court of Rome, concluding with the usual appeal to the Future Oecumenical Council.

The spirit of the letter, Neale writes, is summed up in a quotation which it makes from St Augustine: "We suffer injuries with patience, to preserve the peace of the Church; we abhor to yield to any novelty of heresy or schism; we use our utmost efforts to re-enter that external communion from which it is endeavoured to exclude us."[3]

Neale notes that the archbishop and his two suffragans protested against the papal bull *Ineffabilis Deus* of 1854, which made the dogma of the Immaculate Conception of the Blessed Virgin Mary *de fide*.[4] He concludes his account of the Church of Utrecht with the following words:

It seems to me that the little remnant of this afflicted Church are [*sic*] reserved for happier days. Wherever and whenever that Oecumenical

[1] Ibid., pp. 348f.   [3] Ibid., p. 359.
[2] Ibid., p. 358.   [4] Ibid., p. 374.

Council may be, or whatever other means God shall employ to restore the lost unity of Christendom, the labours, and trials, and sufferings of this communion will not be forgotten. Marvellously raised up as she was when human help seemed at an end, marvellously preserved through five years of extreme danger in the present century, her existence once hanging on the steadiness of the gripe by which a drowning prelate was held above water, she can scarcely have been thus maintained that her end should be without honour, that she should dwindle and dwindle until her last spark is extinguished.[1]

Thus Neale relates the history of this hard-pressed, gallant little Church down to his own times. It seemed to him something of a miracle that this Church had survived the persecution of Protestants, the intrigues of the Jesuits, and the machinations of the Court of Rome. God must have some special purpose for her. Neale always had a deep sympathy for the persecuted and oppressed, and a profound respect for those who held fast to the truth unflinchingly. The Church of Utrecht fulfilled both these rôles, and she could not have had a better or more sympathetic champion than Neale.

Dr C. B. Moss relates how he first became acquainted with the Old Catholic Church of Holland through reading Neale's book. "The book fascinated me, and I could hardly put it down", he writes.[2] Later on he describes Neale's work as "the standard English authority on the subject ever since, and which is considered by some to be his greatest work".[3]

Neale would be delighted to know that the Church of England now has full intercommunion with the Old Catholic Church of Holland. His labour in this field helped to bring about the reunion, for which he prayed and strove so earnestly.

We have now seen something of Neale's influence in the Church of England in connection with the Roman claims, the Eastern Church, and the Old Catholic Church of Holland. From the survey we have tried to make of his work for reunion, it is clear that he had a truly oecumenical outlook in the primitive sense of that word. He saw as the true basis for unity that which had been accepted by the undivided Church, before the great schism between East and West. But whilst resisting the Roman claims, he saw that there could be no real union without the great Latin Church of the West. He would certainly have resisted

---

[1] Ibid., pp. 380f.　　　[2] Moss, op. cit., p. v.　　　[3] Ibid., p. 330.

any attempt to align the Church of England with a purely Protestant movement towards union. He would also have rejected any reunion with Nonconformists which involved the sacrifice of Church principles. To him the first stage on the road to reunion was agreement between Canterbury and Constantinople, or Canterbury and Utrecht. If he had known that agreement between the latter communions would be achieved seventy-four years after the publication of his book, he would have been devoutly thankful to God that his labour for this cause had not been in vain.

12

Trouble with the Bishop

WHY did the Bishop of Chichester (Ashurst Turner Gilbert, bishop 1842–70) inhibit Neale, not only from ministering in his diocese, but also in Sackville College Chapel, which, as the patrons claimed, was outside his jurisdiction? Mary Lawson, writing about her father to Mrs Towle in 1906, says in parenthesis: "Poor Bishop Gilbert! He will be remembered in the history of his diocese only as the man, who muzzled one of its greatest men."[1]

The story of Neale's inhibition is told at length in the *St Margaret's Magazine* memoir, and also by Mrs Towle.[2] It was claimed by the patrons that Sackville College had always been external to the bishop's jurisdiction. A previous bishop had recognized it as such. We read in the *St Margaret's Magazine*:

> The patrons therefore dissuaded the new warden and chaplain from asking the license, which it was his own wish to have procured. The Bishop had very cordially consented to give a license in 1842, when Mr. Neale was presented to Crawley, and when his writings had already caused his principles to be well known. So there could be little apprehension as to whether he would give one now. But it was not asked out of deference to the patrons' strenuous wish; and this omission lay at the root of much that followed.

Neale evidently anticipated some trouble a few months after his arrival. On 22 June 1846 he wrote in his journal:

> I never should be surprised (and I put it down here, in case the evil should come, when it may be a comfort to me to know that I anticipated it) if, from one side or the other, we have a very considerable storm to conquer. However, we have the right on our side—and that is the comfort.

[1] Unpublished letter.
[2] *Memoir*, pp. 335a–62a. Towle, *Memoir*, pp. 155–64.

The beginning of the trouble was on 20 September 1846. On that date Neale records in his journal:

> Just before dinner some Priest came, a thorough Protestant, who asked Anne (the cook) if this were a "Protestant" or "Popish" College.

In a letter to Benjamin Webb he describes how this visitor, whose name was Hutton, found a Vulgate edition of the Scriptures and a Breviary in the chapel, and remarked that the whole look of the chapel was Popish. This Hutton was an evangelical preacher from Sydenham, who had taken the great house at Felbridge. He left Neale with the words: "Oh! If I were a Bishop I would be down upon you at once."[1]

Hutton evidently informed the bishop, and in the following April Neale had this letter from the bishop:

> Having been informed that you have recently come to reside at Sackville College in East Grinstead, I write to request you that you will have the goodness to communicate with me before you officiate, if it be your wish to officiate, in any Church or Chapel in this diocese.[2]

In reply Neale expressed his grief at the bishop's censure, remarked that he seldom officiated in the diocese of Chichester, and said that, notwithstanding the exemption of the College, he had been anxious to have the bishop's licence, but had followed the wishes of the patrons in not applying for one.

In May the bishop held a Confirmation in the parish church of East Grinstead, and after the service visited Sackville College Chapel. He was accompanied by Hutton. The result of the bishop's visit was that Neale was inhibited "from celebrating Divine Worship, and from the exercise of clerical functions" in the diocese of Chichester. The complaint against Neale was the simple furnishing of the chapel, which was described by the bishop as "frippery". He was accused of transforming "the simplicity of the chapel at Sackville College into an imitation of the degrading superstitions of an erroneous Church".[3]

Neale evidently took the inhibition to mean that he might carry on the services in the college chapel, whilst abstaining from officiating anywhere else in the diocese. The bishop, however, intended the inhibition to include the college chapel.

---

[1] *Letters*, p. 99.   [2] *Memoir*, p. 344a.   [3] Ibid., p. 347a.

On 12 May 1847 the bishop wrote to the churchwardens of
East Grinstead informing them of the inhibition, and asking
them to make inquiries "whether Mr Neale obeys the inhibition,
or continues to officiate there".[1] One of the churchwardens,
however, refused to reply to the bishop's inquiries on the ground
that he would not act as a spy. The other on the principle of
obedience to the bishop collected what information he could.
In the meantime Neale carried on in the normal way at the
chapel.

Six months later,

On the 14th November 1847 the Warden received intimation that
articles were to be exhibited against him in the Court of Arches (the
cause being transferred thither by letters of request from the
Bishop's own Court), for administering the Holy Communion, for
preaching, and for publicly reading prayers, in a certain unconsecrated
building commonly known as Sackville Chapel, notwithstanding
an inhibition on the part of the Bishop of Chichester.[2]

The patron, Lord De La Warr, tried to satisfy the bishop by
offering to have removed, with the concurrence of the warden,
such decorations from the chapel as might be thought objectionable. The bishop, however, in his reply to his lordship on 23
January 1848 wrote:

When I state that my view is that I am bound to endeavour to effect
the removal, or the silencing of Mr Neale in my Diocese, if practicable, either immediately, or at no distant time, your Lordship
will perceive that I cannot entertain a hope that the conference
proposed between the legal advisers on either side will lead to a
conclusion to which I could give my consent. . . .[3]

When Lord De La Warr urged that even if the bishop was
successful the warden would not be removed, and the only
difference would be that the aged pensioners would be deprived
of the ministrations of a clergyman and the weekly Communion,
the bishop replied that he could not help the consequences, and
the suit went on.

The case was heard before the Court of Arches on 3 June 1848.
The defence was that Mr Neale was bound by the statutes of the
college to read prayers morning and evening. These prayers were
strictly private, being confined to the inmates of the college and
such friends as might be visitors. The Holy Communion had

[1] Ibid., p. 349a.   [2] Ibid., p. 350a.   [3] Ibid., p. 351a.

been celebrated without a licence, because a licence was believed to be unnecessary. There was a tradition 240 years old that the college chapel was outside the jurisdiction of the bishop.

The bishop's case was that the college chapel could not be shown to be, according to the 71st Canon, "dedicated and allowed according to the Ecclesiastical Laws of this Realm". In spite of this the Holy Communion had been celebrated and sermons preached in it. The Charter (which apparently was not produced) was of no account to the Court.[1]

It was no doubt a foregone conclusion that the case would go against Neale, who by then was numbered amongst the "Puseyites". In a letter to Webb dated 20 July 1847, Neale had said: "We have got into battle with the managers of the *soi-disant* national school here, who would not receive my wife's subscription, because she is a Puseyite."[2] Vincent Neale, writing about his father many years later, said:

> The term "Puseyite" during the forties and fifties involved the greatest detestation through all England; sensible level-headed men were "Pusey" mad. I know not whether it was my father, or some friend of his, who being urged to seek legal redress for some outrageous attack or slander refused to do so saying, "It is useless; there is not a jury in the whole of England, who would render a verdict in favor of a so-called 'Puseyite'"; and this was true as many examples had proved.[3]

The judgement of the Court of Arches was that Mr Neale was liable to ecclesiastical censure, but the Court would be satisfied with admonishing him to abstain from officiating in future without due authority, that authority being the licence of the bishop. Mr Neale was to bear the costs of the proceedings.[4]

On the same day Webb, when he had heard the result, wrote to Neale:

> You never told me the time of the trial. I got there soon after 11, and was late. . . . Neither of the advocates, nor the judge, got up the case. . . . I never heard such astounding ignorance on all sides: such a mockery of justice. There was not a single good thing said on either side. I think Fust meant to be fair; and if the Statutes had been produced and I had been your advocate, you would have established

[1] Ibid., pp. 353a ff.
[2] *Letters*, p. 103.
[3] Article by Vincent Neale, *St Margaret's Half-Yearly Chronicle*, July 1918.
[4] *Memoir*, pp. 354a ff.

the right of reading prayers. It seems to me that you may now exclude the Collegians, keep the Chapel key, and use it for your own oratory:—and no great loss.

On the next day Neale wrote to his wife:

You will have heard from B.W. this morning the result of the trial. Remember that "It is not ignominious to be wronged". . . .[1]

During the next few months several attempts were made to get the bishop to withdraw the inhibition. On 26 March 1849 Neale, in view of the fact that Holy Week and Easter were approaching, wrote a most conciliatory letter to the bishop appealing to him to withdraw the inhibition, at any rate as far as the college was concerned. He concludes with these words:

I appeal to your Lordship's generosity, because the power is entirely on your side; to your Lordship's sense of justice, because a year's suspension is considered sufficient punishment for very flagrant offences; to your Lordship's dealings in similar cases, for few Clergymen coming for institution could produce higher testimonials than those which Lord De La Warr submitted to you; and lastly, if your Lordship has felt hurt, or has been injured, either by the lawsuit, or by any behaviour of mine—to your remembrance of Him Who at this time set us an example of forgiving: and on all these grounds I ask your Lordship, as earnestly as a man ever asked anything, to allow me, on what conditions you please, to officiate in this place (I say nothing of the diocese in general), it being clearly in your Lordship's power at any moment to withdraw that permission, and to restore the present state of things.[2]

The bishop replied two days later with a curt note, in which he said: "Nothing has occurred in the interval since my last reply to alter the position in which respectively we are placed."[3]

In spite of the fact that representations were made to the bishop on Neale's behalf both by Lord De La Warr and Bishop Wilberforce, and a petition was presented to the bishop by the pensioners and inmates of Sackville College, the inhibition was not withdrawn until about 1863. Thus for fifteen years Neale was inhibited by the bishop of the diocese in which he resided. As no definite reason was given for the infliction of the sentence, so none was given for its removal.[4]

Looking back on these events to-day, it is perhaps not difficult for us to understand Bishop Gilbert's attitude to Neale. Before

[1] Ibid., pp. 355a ff.   [3] Ibid., p. 358a.
[2] Ibid., p. 357a.   [4] Ibid., p. 362a.

being nominated as Bishop of Chichester by Sir Robert Peel in 1842, Dr Gilbert was Principal of Brasenose College, Oxford. He held this post for twenty years. Sir John Otter in his *Memoir of Nathaniel Woodard* writes of him as follows:

> He was resident at Oxford during the great years of the Catholic movement. He did not join in it. Though rather clearly defined as a high churchman he probably regarded it with some suspicion. . . . He was a man of culture and polished manners; open minded; kind to all; quite pervious to new ideas, sustaining the great reforms of his predecessor William Otter.[1]

Bishop Gilbert supported Woodard in his work for schools, though somewhat cautiously. Sir John Otter describes a rowdy meeting at the Town Hall, Brighton, on 2 December 1856, which had been arranged in support of St Nicholas' College, Lancing. There was some organized opposition to the meeting by the ultra-Protestants. The bishop, who was to move the resolution supporting the project, was actually accused of being a Puseyite in disguise, and was severely heckled by the opposition:

> Dr Gilbert, notwithstanding the novel experience of facing a storm of howls, catcalls, and insults, courageously delivered a long speech. Nor was his personal appearance spared. It was his habit to articulate precisely each syllable, and when he referred to his e-pis-co-pate, a voice cried, "What pate? Your bald pate, you mean".[2]

Isaac Williams has something to say about Dr Gilbert in his autobiography. He had led the opposition against Isaac Williams' candidature for the Poetry Professorship at Oxford in 1842:

> Dr Gilbert had become head of the anti-Tractarian party . . . but in some degree accidentally, and not altogether owing to difference in principle. When Newman went abroad in 1832–3, and left me in charge of St Mary's, Dr Gilbert and Mrs Gilbert were very kind to me, and admired Newman very much. Mrs Gilbert told me long after that Dr Gilbert always bought her, as his own present, every book that Newman wrote; but he afterwards took offence, chiefly from things said in St Mary's pulpit. . . . The Principal was an extremely irritable person, and became very hostile to Newman, and in consequence, when the contest for this election took place, took a very active lead against us. But after all his opposition was mainly, as against Newman's friend, rather than grounded on a great antagonism of principles.[3]

[1] Sir John Otter, *Nathaniel Woodard* (1925), pp. 49f.
[2] Ibid., p. 111.
[3] *The Autobiography of Isaac Williams*, edited by the Ven. Sir George Prevost (1893), p. 145.

Though Dr Gilbert's leanings were in favour of high church opinions, he was against any approach to Romanism, and what he considered to be Romanizing ceremonial. In 1868 he took legal proceedings against the Reverend John Purchas for ritualistic services at St James's Chapel, Brighton. It seems that the bishop was incited by Protestant agitators (Hutton was such a one), and was really afraid of Neale and what he stood for. Neale was quite fearless, and when he knew he was right, and on the side of the truth, nothing would move him. In controversy he could be a devastating opponent.

In 1852, some four years after the inhibition order, Neale published anonymously an open letter to the Lord Bishop of Chichester entitled *Pictorial Crucifixes*, and signed it, "A Priest of the Diocese". There is little doubt that Bishop Gilbert must have guessed who the anonymous priest was. Certainly the letter did not pour oil on troubled waters, but Neale did not intend that it should. He was fighting for the truth.

The letter is worth quoting at some length, because it is a good example of Neale's skill in debate. The bishop had written an open letter to the incumbent of St Paul's, Brighton (The Reverend A. D. Wagner), condemning the use of pictures of a crucifix. The letter was entitled "Pictorial Crucifixes", and had evidently been prompted by Brighton Protestants.

Neale in his reply, by way of introduction, claims to have been acquainted with Brighton for thirty years. He continues:

As one who has admired your Lordship's stand in defence of Synodical action and the freedom of Church education, I am the more deeply grieved at the tone and teaching of this, the last production of your pen. In what I have to say, I hope I shall remember that I am speaking, a Priest to a Bishop: but neither can I forget that Bishop and Priest are bound to receive one common faith, have sworn to obey one common Church, and have to expect one common reckoning in the great day of account. If, therefore, I am persuaded that the teaching of your Lordship's letter is opposed to Holy Scripture—perilous to the salvation of those poor, to whom, above others, the Gospel is preached,—and if logically carried out, endangering . . . any possibility of a realization of the doctrine of the Incarnation; then I am bound by my Ordination vow, earnestly to contend, let who will be its attacker, for the Faith once for all delivered to the Saints.

First of all Neale criticizes the title, "Pictorial Crucifixes".

Why not call them "Pictures of the Crucifixion"? He quotes a story about Charles Simeon:

> A young composer of sermons was reading a discourse. . . . At length the flow of his eloquence reached the following passage: "Amidst the tumult and outcry of the children of Israel, the son of Amram stood unmoved." "The son of Amram!", interrupted Simeon, "The son of Amram! Who was he?" "Why, sir, I meant Moses." "Then", thundered the critic, "if you *meant* Moses, sir, why not *say* Moses?" I fancy I see the venerable old man now, with his bluff and decided, and yet good humoured manner—"If he meant a picture of the Crucifixion, why not say a picture of the Crucifixion?"

Neale goes on to show that the term "pictorial crucifix" was invented by the Brighton Protestant Defence Committee, which was "composed in about equal numbers of professing Churchmen and real Dissenters". He continues:

> The greater part of your Lordship's pages is occupied by an attempt to prove that pictorial representations, as a means of quickening spiritual devotion, are forbidden by the letter of the Old, and by the spirit of the New Testament. My Lord, you have appealed to Scripture, and to Scripture you shall go.

But before going to Scripture Neale refers to the necessity of pictures in teaching the poor and ignorant. He cites the case of a labourer, a regular attendant at church, who, when shown a picture of the Crucifixion, exclaimed: "What! You don't mean to say that they fastened Him up with nails to a Cross alive? . . . Poor thing, how it must have hurt Him!" This man, Neale asserts, but for one of these "pictorial crucifixes" would have remained ignorant of how our salvation was brought to pass to his dying day. He then continues:

> Thus, by the forbidding of such pictorial representations, one great means of instruction is closed to the poor. . . . Your argument in fact is: The rich do not want them, and therefore the poor shall not have them. You would spiritualize their feelings, utterly forgetful that the whole system of their education renders them utterly inaccessible, except through material objects. You have no sympathy with them in their grossness and dullness of their intellect, and therefore treat them—oh how differently from Him Who knew what was in man!

Neale then turns to the main argument that the awakening of devotion by pictorial representation is unscriptural:

Your Lordship says, "If at any time such aids and helps have been expedient, may we not believe God in His mercy would have directed man towards them? But where in the whole Bible is there any command or suggestion of the kind? You can point to neither text nor circumstance bearing that way." I accept your Lordship's challenge. I say that the New Testament is full, to a degree which *a priori* we could not have expected, of teaching by pictorial representations. I do not say that our Blessed Lord or His Apostles distributed to the poor these pictures, which your Lordship so accurately describes; or that a miracle was wrought to produce symbols, which before the invention of the printing press could only thus have been created. But looking at the general character and spirit of our Blessed Lord's teaching, will you dare to deny that it was essentially carried on, not by the mere dead sermon-like statement of facts, but by the living teaching of living pictures? "Lift up your eyes and look upon the fields, for they are white already to harvest." Is not that a pictorial representation? Does it matter one straw to the argument whether it were taken from the printed leaf of a book, or from the great field of nature? . . . Will anyone venture to say that, had prints in our sense of the word been then known, our Lord Who drew so vivid a picture to the ear, would not gladly, to speak with all reverence, have availed Himself of that means of representing it to the eye? In fact, when I think of the numberless parables and illustrations which are pictures, or which are nothing . . . I am constrained to say, that if there be such a thing as clear and definite teaching in Scripture, then your Lordship's assertion, which I have just quoted, is as unscriptural as anything I ever remember to have read.

Neale also reminds the bishop of our Lord "going down to the porch of the temple and directing the attention of His disciples to the vine moulding, which we know from Jewish testimony to have formed its cornice", and saying "I am the true Vine. . . ."

He next considers the bishop's reference to the Second Commandment, and points out that the bishop's comment on it, whether taken literally or spiritually, is most unscriptural.

If taken literally the Second Commandment forbids two things:
(1) the making any pictorial representation of any animal whatever;
(2) the falling down and worshipping it.

According to such literal interpretation "all pictures or sculptures of men or beasts are forbidden; and I regret to say that your Lordship's carriage, decorated as it is with a Prester John, seated on a tombstone, is a standing infraction of the second Commandment."

Reference is then made to something which Dr Arnold has

said on the subject. Whilst Neale carefully guards himself against any suggestion of agreeing with Dr Arnold's general teaching, he says:

> But one great truth I conceive him to have stated most strikingly and most plainly; namely, that the very fact of the Incarnation abrogates, in its literal sense, the second Commandment. It would be as reasonable, since the Resurrection, to insist on the literal observance of the fourth Commandment, and the hallowing of the Saturday, as it is, since the Incarnation, to demand literal compliance with the second, and the abstaining from all representations connected with Divine worship. . . . And hence the intimate connection between Christian art, and the doctrine of the Incarnation. As by uniting it to His Godhead, never to be thence divided, He hallowed matter; so, by the same deed, He consecrated material representations. This, if viewed philosophically, is no vain question; it is no disputing about matters of taste; it is a want of grasp over the main article of the Christian Truth. Hence the jealous care with which pictures have been guarded and contended for. . . .

Neale then takes up the bishop's assertion that the Reformed Communions have rejected such things altogether:

> Now these few words involve a question very seriously regarding your Lordship's character as a controversialist. By the Reformed Communions, technically speaking, Calvinistic bodies are meant; of them the assertion is true. But it will popularly be taken to mean all Protestants, and then it is utterly false. Lutherans, as every traveller is aware, not only use crucifixes, but images of saints; deck them with garlands of flowers, and burn tapers before them. I will not believe that your Lordship meant to write a sentence which is true in one sense, but false in that in which you knew it would generally be taken. I cannot believe that. I may see carelessness, thoughtlessness, recklessness, in other assertions; but God forbid that I should attribute to you the desire to deceive, and that by an assertion, which, on account of its partial truth, would be the worst of falsehoods. But there is only one alternative: the assertion must be made from the grossest ignorance. You must have believed that Lutherans rejected images. But in that case, you could neither have visited their churches nor read their books. What then are we to think of the confidence with which you make an assertion respecting their uses, when into those uses you had never enquired, and by consequence knew nothing of them?

Neale then accuses Dr Gilbert of being the first English bishop to condemn pictorial representations of our Lord, and asks if it is not remarkable that "this great truth, hidden till now, should be revealed to you? for indeed, if it be true, it is scarcely less than a new revelation". It ought to be such to warrant his passing by so contemptuously "the work of faith, and labour of love, and patience . . . so conspicuous in St Paul's". Neale deplores the envy, hatred, and uncharitableness which the bishop's letter will let loose in Brighton. "Your Lordship has fanned the almost extinguished ashes into a blaze."

In his last paragraph but one, Neale says that he is informed that the bishop "intends to appeal to public opinion in a second and third letter on the subject of Confession and the Holy Eucharist". Neale warns the bishop: "As each of these letters appear I purpose to trouble your Lordship with a few remarks upon it." Neale concludes by saying that none of the St Paul's clergy are in the slightest degree responsible for what has been written.

The bishop, when he read this letter,[1] must have felt somewhat deflated. Neale had not spared any punches, and, except to the blindly prejudiced, the bishop must have appeared rather foolish; but his logic would not dispose the bishop to regard him in a more favourable light. Be that as it may, the bishop does not seem to have attempted to cross swords with Neale again: the proposed letters on Confession and the Holy Eucharist apparently did not appear. Thus it would seem that Neale effectively silenced his bishop on these subjects.

It is good to know, however, that Samuel Wilberforce, the Bishop of Oxford, recognized Neale's great gifts and stood by him on a number of occasions. It was probably through him that the Bishop of Chichester was finally persuaded to withdraw his inhibition. Neale wrote to Webb on 19 September 1856:

> I was at Lavington with the Bishop of Oxford for two nights. He told me that Chichester, in talking to him about me, said, "It is very true that there was some unpleasantness between Mr Neale and myself some time ago, but that is all over now, except that I am afraid he believes in Transubstantiation."[2]

Some seven years later he was able to write:

> It is really providential that now, about three weeks ago, the Bishop *formally*, as he did three years ago *virtually* withdrew his inhibition; so, I hope, ends a battle of more than sixteen years; I having not

[1] *Pictorial Crucifixes: A Letter to the Lord Bishop of Chichester.* By a Priest of the Diocese (1852).
[2] *Letters,* p. 277.

withdrawn a single word nor altered a single practice (except by way of going further). . . .[1]

Neale completed his reconciliation with the bishop by dedicating his collection of Seatonian Prize Poems to him.

Bishop Wilberforce's sympathy with Neale is shown by the following incident. When the new railway between Tunbridge Wells and East Grinstead was opened on 18 July 1864, there was a banquet at which Bishop Wilberforce was the guest of honour. Neale was not invited. At the head of the table the Bishop asked, "Where is Neale?" It is not known what answer he was given, but immediately after the dinner he went straight to Sackville College to call on the man who had not been invited to meet him.[2]

---

[1] Ibid., p. 328; also Towle, *Memoir*, p. 299. Mrs. Lawson dates the formal withdrawal of the bishop's inhibition in 1860, whereas Towle, *Memoir*, has 1863. The latter would seem to be correct.

[2] Towle, *Memoir*, pp. 269f.

13

The Man and his Achievement

WE have now traced Neale's influence in Church Architecture, the revival of the Religious Life, Hymnology, and Reunion. We have seen that he was the chief founder of the Cambridge Camden Society. There was hardly a church in this country, in the latter half of the nineteenth century, which was not affected in some way by this Society. Numerous churches were restored, and many new ones built, in accordance with its principles: in fact, never before had the Church of England seen so much church restoration and building. Moreover the influence of the Society was felt far beyond England: it affected the whole Anglican Communion and beyond. In its early years Neale was not only its guiding hand, but also its driving force.

Though Neale was not the first to bring about a revival of the Religious Life in the Church of England in the nineteenth century, he showed that he had a clearer grasp of the requirements of monasticism than many of his contemporaries. He saw what was necessary for the stability of a religious community, and he built the Society of St Margaret upon sure foundations. Even members of the Russian Church came to him for advice about forming Sisterhoods for active work in the world.

His masterly translations of Latin hymns convinced the doubtful that vernacular hymns had a place in Anglican worship. The use of these hymns during the past hundred years or so has shown the superiority of Neale's over other translations. His translations and paraphrases of Greek hymns opened up an entirely new store of ancient hymns to the Western Church. His original hymns, on the whole, are probably not of equal merit to his translations, but a number have won a lasting place in the hymnody of the Church.

Neale was convinced of the catholicity of the Church of

England, and longed for her unity with the rest of Catholic Christendom. He was not impressed by the Roman claims, and saw the weaknesses of the Roman system. He looked rather to the East and to Holland for the ideal of the Catholic Church. He felt that the first stage in reunion would be some rapprochement between Canterbury and Constantinople, or Canterbury and Utrecht. He helped to break down the insularity of the Church of England of the nineteenth century, and put both the Eastern Church and the Church of Holland on the map for English churchpeople.

Reference has been made earlier to his influence in the ceremonial revival. From the earliest days of his work with the Cambridge Camden Society, Neale was convinced that the revival of church architecture would bring about a revival of Catholic ceremonial in the Church. He gave a lead to this to some extent in Sackville College Chapel, but much more so in St Margaret's Oratory, the private chapel of the Sisters. Here he was one of the first to revive the use of the eucharistic vestments. Here he had most of the externals which one would expect to see in an Anglo-Catholic church to-day—altar lights, sanctuary lamps, stations of the Cross, the use of incense, and of course Reservation. The dignity of Anglican worship to-day, which is now largely taken for granted in all schools of thought, is due to the work of pioneers like Neale.

In this very inadequate estimate of a great priest's work and influence little so far has been said of his character. The kind of man he was is shown to some extent in the work which he undertook and accomplished so well. Before we consider his character we may give a friend's description of his appearance:

He was a tall, angular, rather loosely-limbed man, dressed in the old-fashioned way that Pusey, and Keble, and Isaac Williams used to dress, in swallow-tailed coats, tall hats, and white ties. He was sallow in complexion, with dark and not very tidily brushed hair, short-sighted, wore spectacles, and had a distraught and dreamy look, as though his thoughts were far away. His head was intellectual, and when a smile crossed his somewhat melancholic aspect, it animated his entire features, like a sunbeam on a winter's day. Within the College precincts, and at the Sisterhood, he always dressed in his cassock, with a trencher cap on his head, and a pair of bands under his chin.[1]

---

[1] George Huntington, *Random Recollections* (1896), p. 206.

The first thing that stands out in his life is his faith in God and his Church. He never wrote the word *God* without underlining it twice. He had a deep devotion to our Lord, which is shown in his reverence for him in the Blessed Sacrament and in his daily use of the Litany of the Holy Name. He had a profound knowledge of the Scriptures, and was thoroughly versed in their mystical interpretation. To him the whole of the Bible from beginning to end was about Christ. He found great inspiration in the lives of the saints and martyrs, and loved relating their histories. He was convinced that the Church of England was a true part of the One Holy Catholic and Apostolic Church founded by Christ. She had a valid ministry and sacraments, and was God's instrument for the salvation of this country. If only men were loyal to her teaching, as seen against the background of the whole Church Catholic, all would be well.

Like most of the saints he had his moments of depression and doubt. After the riot at Lewes he wrote to Webb:

> I don't think, however, that I ever suffered so much as in these last ten days. However innocent, or rather, however right, one may know oneself to be, it is not pleasant to be posted over England as a rascal.[1]

On another occasion, writing to encourage a friend, he reveals something of his own inner suffering which at times came upon him:

> I think that even you have no idea—and yet you have more idea than anyone else—how much I suffer from this persecution against the College; how it distracts my thoughts in prayer; how it hinders my rest; how (for I am speaking to you without any reserve) it would tempt me, unless I were very watchful, to think that God is suffering me to be tempted above what I am able to bear. But, though all this is so, I am not discouraged, as though my feeling the thing so bitterly were any reason for my believing that I were less in earnest in serving God. . . .[2]

Any depression or doubt, however, which he might feel at times, was soon over. He stood as firm as a rock in his convictions, and nothing would daunt him.

Although he was never very robust in health, he never spared himself. He worked long hours. In the early days of the Sisterhood he would sometimes walk the fourteen miles from East Grinstead

[1] *Letters*, p. 299.   [2] Towle, *Memoir*, p. 227.

to Rotherfield and back. As the victim of riots on several occasions, he showed remarkable physical courage. At one time his house at East Grinstead was nearly set on fire by an unruly mob. His experience at Lewes would have shaken many men stronger than he, but at the time he hardly seems to have turned a hair. To him it was all part of Christian witness. The martyrs of old had experienced much worse treatment.

Though he had strong views and opinions, and was not afraid to express them—especially when unpopular—he was by nature extremely shy and reticent. The writer of his obituary notice in the *Church Review* describes him, as a small child, creeping under the sofa when anybody came to call. Later on, when he was old enough to go to school, it was an understood thing that no one should be invited to the house during his holidays. One wonders how his sensitive nature stood up to the rough and tumble of Victorian school life. When he reached manhood, he still retained a reserve towards strangers, which was noticeable to the last. The Reverend George Huntington compares Neale with John Keble:

> The two men were much alike in their reserve and dislike of notoriety. But Neale was at times so abstracted and absorbed that it was no easy matter to draw him out. Stories are told of people, who made pilgrimages to the picturesque and quaint old College, to interview him, as the Yankees say, and who went back with hardly the inter-change of a word. But when visitors properly accredited came, they found him a man of infinite resources.[1]

He was no time-server, and always refused to compromise. Some light is thrown on this side of his character by Webb in his account of the relationship between Neale and A. J. Beresford Hope. The latter was a leading layman of the Church, a member of the Cambridge Camden Society, and a Member of Parliament. For a time Neale wrote articles for the *Morning Chronicle*, in which Hope had an interest. Webb often had to act as a mediator between the two. In a letter to Webb in 1846, Neale asserted that it was "impossible for a man, unless he lives a truly ascetic life, to move in the rank in which he (Hope) moves, and to mix with high life without being infected with the miserable compromising spirit of the day".

Hope, on the other hand, sometimes lost his temper with Neale. He wrote to Webb in 1862:

[1] Huntington, op. cit., p. 198.

Neale is distinguished morally by a combination of tuft-hunting and bristling democracy, a great theoretic admiration of episcopacy with a gift of insulting all embodied Bishops. His veracity is conditioned. Intellectually his faith leads him greedily to swallow all modern forms of credulity, rapping, spiritualism etc. His historical lore, which is great, is altogether subservient to his own one-sided propagandism. Within his own wilful limits he is versatile. Politically he always takes up any cause or interest, which is emphatically and patently un- or anti-English. Personally he is tall and lank and hawk-faced; he snuffles and talks through his nose, and he preferentially wears at all hours tail dress-coats.[1]

This diatribe was obviously written in a fit of pique, but it shows Neale's adamant and uncompromising nature, and how exasperating he could be at times to those who disagreed with him.

In spite of his refusal to compromise and his strict adherence to his principles Neale was not altogether intolerant of those who differed from him. He was always ready to forgive those who had harmed him, however much he had suffered. It is related that on one occasion, when a former friend turned against him and caused him much trouble and suffering, he went into the chapel of Sackville College and shut himself up there for hours, until he felt he could fully forgive the man.[2]

Neale, of course, had great enthusiasm, which must have been infectious. It was his zeal and energy which launched the Cambridge Camden Society and the Society of St Margaret. Fortunately also he had a sense of humour, which made the setbacks and troubles of his life a little more tolerable. His humour was shown especially in his own family and with close friends. The following letter was written to his son, Cornelius Vincent, when he was six years old and staying with his grandmother, after a serious illness:

Dear Little Cor,

I have written before in prose each day what I had to say: I choose this time to write in rhyme, in hopes that my letter will be much better. We had hoped to-day that the wet was away; but now the rain has begun again. The room we gave Mrs Nichols to have, was so full of fleas and things like these that they scrubbed the floor and they washed the door, cleaned the window-seat and the carpet beat:

---

[1] *Letters*, p. 93. H. W. Law and Irene Law, *The Book of the Beresford Hopes* (1925), p. 145.
[2] Towle, *Memoir*, p. 164.

but the more they could do the worse it grew. They sent to tell Mr Morell: and then they took the pains to look behind the prints of the sofa chinz: when lo and behold there were more than could be told of great fleas and small fleas and short fleas and tall fleas and slow fleas and quick fleas and well fleas and sick fleas. Morell then said, while he scratched his head, "I must take away this sofa to-day". But Mrs Morell began to yell; and said, "Arthur, dear, it shan't come here". But still, he sent and away it went, and now, if you please, I have done with my fleas, and lay down my pen. Your Papa, J.M.N.[1]

In December 1846 he wrote to Webb describing the setting up of the rood screen in Sackville College Chapel:

Just as the Cross was raised for the first time, the door opened, and in walked a Protestant clergyman. His disgust rendered him speechless for some time. Then he burst forth.

> It would have moved a Christian's bowels
> To hear the doubts he stated;
> But the carpenters did
> As they were bid,
> And worked the whilst he prated.

The following recollection of Huntington, who is writing about Neale's study, also reveals something of his humour:

Here too, long after the aged pensioners were snoring in their dormitories, he remained until he took his nightly rounds in the quadrangle before retiring for some four hours' sleep. He used to take his friends out to hear the inmates snore. I shall not forget the sounds.[2]

According to his friends he had little idea of money, and gave to beggars quite indiscriminately.[3] He must have had some private means. He could hardly have supported his family on the meagre income of £28 a year which he received as Warden of Sackville College, supplemented though it was by his output of literary work. Mrs Neale was evidently an extremely good economist. According to their son Vincent, she was the family and college treasurer and accountant.[4] Apart from the household and college, there were also the financial responsibilities of the Society of St Margaret when it started.

Though he was so shy with people, he had a wonderful way with children. His own children adored him, and in spite of his

[1] *St Margaret's Quarterly* (Boston, Mass., U.S.A.), Summer 1955.
[2] Huntington, op. cit., p. 205.
[3] Ibid., p. 201.
[4] *St Margaret's Quarterly* (Boston, Mass., U.S.A.), Summer 1955.

manifold labours, he found time to take them for walks, and to thrill them with stories. His son writes:

In spite of his multifarious work my father found time for family pleasures and intercourse; every Sunday afternoon, when fine, he walked out with his children, and often at other times; every summer had its picnics on the birthday of some member, which took them all out for the day. During the long winter evenings he would sometimes supervise a game of chess, and would at other times read aloud.[1]

As special treats there were visits to fairs and circuses. In the case of the latter he always called on the proprietor beforehand, in order to satisfy himself that there would be nothing in the performance unsuitable for children. On one occasion when the proprietor could not guarantee this, he sent up his elephants *gratis* to perform in the quadrangle of Sackville College, to the great delight of the children and inmates.[2] He devoted also much time to the children of the orphanage, and many of his children's stories were written for them.

He had a deep sympathy with the animal creation. Huntington relates that on a visit to Tarporley in the last year of his life, when the cattle plague was on, he was found on his knees in the cowhouses praying for the suffering animals. It was at this time that he wrote his Cattle Plague hymn.[3] When he was in Madeira, he had a dog called Pombal, who was his constant companion. When the dog died, he never had another, but for about eight years he went on marking in his diary the number of days since Pombal's death.[4]

Finally we must mark the thoroughness with which Neale tackled every task. We have noted this in his work on hymns, with the Sisters, and with reunion. It was true of all his undertakings—"Whatsoever thy hand findeth to do, do it with thy might" was a favourite text.

Neale had little recognition from the Church of England of his own day, in spite of his manifold labours for the Church. As we have seen he was inhibited for the greater part of his time at Sackville College by the Bishop of Chichester. But whilst he was a prophet without honour in his own country, he did not go

[1] *St Margaret's Half-Yearly Chronicle* (East Grinstead), July 1918.
[2] *Letters*, p. 339.
[3] Huntington, op. cit., p. 201.
[4] *Letters*, p. 353.

unrecognized in other countries. As we have seen, he was much thought of by leading men of the Russian Church. His work was even acknowledged by the Emperor himself. Another part of the world which valued his work was the United States of America. In 1860 he received an honorary D.D. degree from Trinity College, Hartford, Connecticut. The announcement of the awarding of this degree was communicated to one of his friends as follows:

> I am able to gratify you and myself by announcing that Neale is D.D. of Trinity College, Hartford. The degree was conferred in a beautiful form: "For the glory of God and the benefit of His Holy Church" etc., and when it came to *In Nomine Patris* etc. all rose and said "Amen". In none of our other Colleges is this solemnity observed. . . . At the dinner, in reply to a toast, I thanked the members of the Corporation for having honoured *themselves* by being the first to pay this deserved compliment to a scholar among the first of his age. The members of Convocation responded to this by loud cheers, and I assured them they should know how Dr Neale had received it.[1]

It was some encouragement to Neale to know that his work was appreciated in some places.

The earthly remains of Neale lie at the south-east corner of the churchyard of the parish church of St Swithun, East Grinstead. His grave is almost opposite to the entrance of the original St Margaret's Convent. In that group of buildings, now completely altered and used mostly as shops, Neale's greatest work (as he himself would have said), the fostering of the Society of St Margaret, was patiently and devotedly carried on. In the middle of that block is an old wooden building with a corrugated iron roof. In the old days this building joined the Sisters' quarters with the orphanage. Here was St Margaret's Oratory, the heart of the convent. Here in a room, described as long and narrow, which had once been a workshop, the Blessed Sacrament was reserved for probably the first time in the nineteenth century in the Church of England, and in a tabernacle on the altar. Here his sermons on the Religious Life—surely some of the finest in the English language—were preached.[2]

To the north-east of the old convent lies Sackville College. There the chapel can be seen to-day largely as Neale left it, with its rood screen, stone altar, and stained-glass east window in

---

[1] Towle, *Memoir*, p. 280.
[2] Mother Kate, *Memories of a Sister of St Saviour's Priory* (1903), p. 22.

memory of his father. Leading out of the chapel on the north side is a small study with two windows east and west. The eastern one looks out on Ashdown Forest, the western one on the college quadrangle. It was from the view of the former that his first thoughts about the Sisterhood came. In Neale's day, of course, this study was lined with shelves and numerous books. Here he carried on his literary work, standing at a high desk. Beyond the study lay the warden's house.

The real memorial to Neale is the present St Margaret's Convent, which lies about half a mile to the north-west of Sackville College, off Moat Road. The foundation-stone of these buildings was laid just over a year before he died. He lived to see the walls raised only a few feet. The convent was designed by the eminent Victorian architect, George Edmund Street, who was a personal friend. Mr Peter Anson describes it as "an example of Gothic Revival architecture which no other country in Europe can equal".[1] No doubt the present convent buildings incorporate many of Neale's own ideas. At any rate, his spirit still pervades this mother house of the Society of St Margaret with its affiliated and daughter houses all over the world, and he prays for his spiritual daughters now, even more earnestly and effectively than when he was with them in the flesh.

Neale may have been without much honour in the Church of England of his own times, but to-day, one hundred years later, as we look back on his life and work, we can see what great things he achieved for the Church, which he loved so much, and which in many ways treated him so badly. The Church of England has hardly ever had a more devoted son, and she can certainly never have had one who worked harder in her service. It would seem that no other man ever managed to crowd so much into a day. He had, of course, outstanding natural gifts, a wonderful memory and an extraordinary gift for languages, but he was only able to achieve so much because he was a man of profound faith, prophetic vision, and great spiritual power. His life was indeed "hid with Christ in God".

He departed this life on 6 August 1866, the feast of the Transfiguration, and the day before the feast of the Holy Name, for which he had a special devotion. And it was most fitting that one who in his sermons had spoken so constantly of heaven and

[1] Peter Anson, *The Call of the Cloister* (1955), p. 337.

the unseen world should have died on a day when the Church on earth rejoices in the certainty of heaven and in the glory which shall be revealed.

We conclude this study with a quotation from the introduction to the Sackville College Sermons, which seems to sum up so aptly the life and work of this great priest:

And Sackville College was in itself a not unsuitable home for such a man. Quiet, withdrawn from the stir and bustle of ordinary life, it was well fitted for the abode of a scholar. That disturbances should in process of time be stirred up, false reports be circulated, and seeds of discord sown, was only to be expected, when the man who was their object was one of the most energetic and untiring restorers of the true doctrine and discipline of the English Church. As he laboured for his College and its little chapel, so, and much more, he laboured for England and its Church. Not rightly appreciated in either case at the time. But over his study door was the inscription: "Through evil report and good report"; and over his mantelpiece: "Per angusta ad augusta". As he once remarked, "he had a good deal of the evil report, and very little of the good". But what matter now? if through the "strait", he has attained to the "high"?[1]

[1] *Sermons Preached in Sackville College Chapel*, vol. i, p. x. The Introduction is anonymous.

Select Bibliography

GENERAL

John Mason Neale, A Memoir: Articles from *St Margaret's Magazine,* 1887–95, bound together in one volume. The numbering of the pages is not consecutive. The anonymous writer of these articles was Sister Miriam, who died in 1923. Cited as *Memoir.*

John Mason Neale, D.D., A Memoir, Eleanor A. Towle. 1906. Cited as Towle, *Memoir.*

Letters of John Mason Neale, D.D., ed. Mary Sackville Lawson. 1910. Cited as *Letters.*

Collected Hymns, Sequences and Carols of John Mason Neale, ed. Mary Sackville Lawson. 1914.

A few unpublished letters and parts of diaries of J. M. Neale at St Margaret's Convent, East Grinstead, Sussex.

A few unpublished letters of Mother Kate (Katherine Anne Egerton Warburton: 1840–1923) at St Saviour's Priory, Haggerston, London E.2.

The Diary of Benjamin Webb (1819–85) at the Bodleian Library, Oxford; MSS. Eng. misc. d.475, e.406–43 and f.97–9.

St Margaret's Magazine (East Grinstead). 1896–1901.

St Margaret's Half-Yearly Chronicle (East Grinstead), especially 1918.

St Margaret's Quarterly (Boston, Mass., U.S.A.), 1955.

Dr Neale, G. Moultrie, reprinted from *The Churchman's Companion.* 1866. Cited as *Dr Neale.*

Random Recollections of Some Noted Bishops, Divines and Worthies of the "Old Church" of Manchester, George Huntington. 1896.

Memories of a Sister of St Saviour's Priory, Mother Kate. 1903.

The Church and the World, Essays on Questions of the Day in 1866, ed. Orby Shipley. 1867.

The Oxford Movement, 1833–1845, R. W. Church. 1891.

The Oxford Movement: Sketches and Recollections, G. Wakeling. 1895.

The Church Revival, S. Baring-Gould. 1914.

A Short History of the Oxford Movement, S. L. Ollard. 1915.

The Story of the Catholic Revival, Clifton Kelway. 1915.

The Oxford Movement and After, C. P. S. Clarke. 1932.

Church and People, 1789–1889, S. C. Carpenter. 1933.

Religion in the Victorian Era, L. E. Elliott-Binns. 1936.

They Shine Like Stars, Desmond Morse-Boycott. 1947.

The Nineteenth Century Country Parson, A. Tindal Hart and Edward Carpenter. 1954.

John Keble, Walter Lock. 1892.

The Life of Edward Bouverie Pusey, H. P. Liddon. 1893.

The Autobiography of Isaac Williams, edited by the Ven. Sir George Prevost. 1893.

The Story of Dr Pusey's Life, by the author of "Charles Lowder". 1900.

The Life of Bishop Wilberforce, vol. i, A. R. Ashwell. 1880 .Vols. ii and iii, R. G. Wilberforce. 1881.

Nathaniel Woodard, Sir John Otter. 1925.

Oxford Apostles, Geoffrey Faber. 1933.

A Dictionary of English Church History, new (third) edition, Ollard, Crosse, and Bond. 1948.

The Oxford Dictionary of the Christian Church, ed. F. L. Cross. 1957.

CHURCH ARCHITECTURE

Bound Volumes of *The Ecclesiologist*, 1841–67. There are twenty-five volumes of the New Series.

Various Pamphlets published by the Cambridge Camden Society (see Appendix to Chapter 4, pp. 37f).

A Memorial of the Cambridge Camden Society, E. J. Boyce. 1888.

A History of the Gothic Revival, Charles L. Eastlake. 1872.

The Book of the Beresford Hopes, Henry William Law and Irene Law. 1925.

Church Builders of the Nineteenth Century, Basil F. L. Clarke. 1938.

The Man of Ten Talents, J. Bromley. 1959.

The Architectural Setting of Anglican Worship, G. W. O. Addleshaw and Frederick Etchells. 1948.

Fashions in Church Furnishings, Peter Anson. 1960.

Liturgy and Architecture, Peter Hammond. 1960.

THE RELIGIOUS LIFE

J. M. Neale's Sermons, especially:
Sermons Preached in a Religious House, 1st series, vols. i and ii; 2nd series, vols. i and ii.

Sermons for the Church Year, vols. i and ii.

Sermons on Passages from the Prophets, vols. i and ii.

Sermons on Passages of the Psalms.

Sermons for Feast Days.

Sermons on the Song of Songs.

Sermons on the Apocalypse.

Sermons on the Blessed Sacrament.

Ayton Priory, or The Restored Monastery, J. M. Neale. 1843.

Sisterhoods of the Church of England, a lecture delivered by The Reverend J. M. Neale. 1865.

The Fundamentals of the Religious State, S. C. Hughson. 1915.

Religious Communities of the Church of England, A. T. Cameron. 1918.

The Call of the Cloister, Peter Anson. 1955.

The Silent Rebellion, A. M. Allchin. 1958.

Priscilla Lydia Sellon, T. J. Williams. 1950.

A Hundred Years of Blessing within an English Community, as recorded by the Community of St Mary the Virgin, Wantage. 1946.

Some Principles of the Religious Life, from the Writings of John Mason Neale. 1956.

HYMNOLOGY

Dictionary of Hymnology, ed. John Julian. 1892.

Hymns Ancient and Modern, Historical Edition. 1909.

Companion to Hymns Ancient and Modern, C. W. A. Brooke. 1914.

Articles by J. M. Neale in the *Christian Remembrancer,* vols. xviii and xlvi.

A Hundred Years of Hymns Ancient and Modern, W. K. Lowther Clarke. 1960.

The Oxford Book of Carols, edited by Percy Dearmer, R. Vaughan Williams, Martin Shaw. 1928.

The English Carol, Erik Routley. 1958.

REUNION

J. M. Neale's Sermons, especially:

Sermons Preached in a Religious House, 1st series, vol. i. 1869.

Occasional Sermons, Preached in Various Churches. 1873.

Lectures on Church Difficulties, with an Introduction by the Reverend W. J. E. Bennett. 1871.

The following works of J. M. Neale:

A History of the Holy Eastern Church—The Patriarchate of Alexandria, 2 vols. 1847.

A History of the Holy Eastern Church—General Introduction, 2 vols. 1850.

Greek Liturgies of SS. Mark, James, Clement, Chrysostom, and Basil. 1859.

English Translation of Greek Liturgies. 1859.

Voices from the East: Documents on the present state and working of the Oriental Church, translated from the original Russ, Slavonic, and French. 1859.

A History of the Holy Eastern Church—The Patriarchate of Antioch, edited by the Reverend George Williams. 1878.

A History of the So-called Jansenist Church of Holland. 1858.

The Union of Christendom, edited by Kenneth Mackenzie. 1938.

The Orthodox Church, Sergius Bulgakov. 1935.

Orthodox Spirituality, A Monk of the Eastern Church. 1945.

The Old Catholic Movement, Its Origin and History, C. B. Moss. 1948.

Christian Unity, The Anglican Position, G. K. A. Bell. 1948.

Appendix

PUBLISHED WORKS OF JOHN MASON NEALE

1841

Account of Restoration in the Church of Old Shoreham, Sussex (T. Stevenson, Cambridge)

The History of Pues (Parker, Rivingtons)

A Few Words to Churchwardens on Churches and Church Ornaments. No. 1, Suited to Country Parishes (Cambridge)

A Few Words to Church Builders (Cambridge)

1842

Supplement to the History of Pues

Bishop Montague's Visitation Articles, with Memoir (Stevenson)

An Historical Outline of the Book of Psalms, by John Mason Good. Edited by J. M. Neale (London)

1843

Church Enlargement and Church Arrangement (Cambridge)

A Few Words to Parish Clerks and Sextons of Country Parishes (Cambridge)

Songs and Ballads for the People (Burns)

The Private Devotions of Bishop Lancelot Andrewes. Part II. Translated from the Latin (Part I, from the Greek, in *Tracts for the Times,* was by J. H. Newman) (Parker)

Hymns for the Sick (Burns, Masters)

Agnes de Tracey: A Tale of the Times of St Thomas of Canterbury (Stevenson, Cambridge)

Ayton Priory, or The Restored Monastery (Rivingtons)

Herbert Tresham: A Story of the Great Rebellion (Rivingtons). Repr. S.P.C.K., 1903

A Song for the Times (Burns, Masters)

Hierologus or the Church Tourists (Burns, Masters). Repr. 1854

Hymns for Children: Series I & II (Burns, Masters)

Symbolism of Churches. Translated from the first book of Durandus, by J. M. Neale and B. Webb (Stevenson)

   3rd Edition, 1906.   French translation, 1847

1844

Letter on Private Devotion in Churches (Burns)

Songs and Ballads for Manufacturers (Burns, Masters)

1845

On the Ecclesiology of Madeira. A paper read before the Cambridge Camden Society (Rivingtons)

English History for Children (Juvenile Englishman's Library: Burns, Masters)
8th edition, 1878

History of Portugal (J.E.L.: Burns)

Triumphs of the Cross: Tales of Christian Heroism (J.E.L.: Burns, Masters). 7th edition, 1882; repr. S.P.C.K., 1902

History of Greece (J.E.L.: Masters)

Shepperton Manor: A Tale of the Times of Bishop Andrewes (Cleaver)
Reprinted by S.P.C.K., 1909

A Mirror of Faith: Lays and Legends of the Church in England (Burns)
A centenary edition with additions, 1918

(In 1845 Neale revised the Portuguese version of the Book of Common Prayer for S.P.C.K.)

1846

Annals of Virgin Saints (Masters)

Illustrations of Monumental Brasses (partly edited by J.M.N.)

Sir Henry Spelman's History and Fate of Sacrilege. Edited by the Revs. J. M. Neale and J. Haskoll. New edition by S. J. Eales, 1888

Stories of the Crusades (Masters)

Triumphs of the Cross: 2nd Series. Tales of Christian Endurance (J.E.L.: Masters). 4th edition, 1872; reprinted by S.P.C.K., 1901

1847

Tales from Heathen Mythology (J.E.L.: Masters). New edition, 1869

Poynings: A Tale of the Revolution (J.E.L.: Masters)

History of the Holy Eastern Church: The Patriarchate of Alexandria. Vols. I and II (Masters, Parker, Macmillan)

The Unseen World: Communications with it, real or imaginary (Burns)
2nd edition, with additions, 1853

1848

Duchenier, or the Revolt of La Vendée (Masters). Repr. S.P.C.K., 1905, 1930

Ecclesiological Notes on the Isle of Man, Ross, Sutherland and the Orkneys (Masters)

"The Ecclesiastical Latin Poetry of the Middle Ages", an Essay in *Encyclopaedia Metropolitana*, Vol. XXV (Griffin)

1849

Tetralogia Liturgica (Leslie)

1850

"The Church's Extremity, her Lord's Opportunity", in *Sermons preached in the Octave of St Barnabas, Pimlico.* Repr. in *Occasional Sermons*, 1873

Documents connected with the Foundation of the Anglican Bishopric in Jerusalem, and with the Protest against Bishop Gobat's Proselytism. Collected and edited by J. M. Neale

1850

Deeds of Faith: Stories for Children from Church History (Mozley)
  2nd edition, 1860; reprinted by S.P.C.K., 1902
A Few Words of Hope on the Present Crisis of the English Church (Masters)
  Two editions in 1850
A Letter to the Ven. Archdeacon Hare with respect to his Pamphlet on the Gorham Question (Masters)
Readings for the Aged (Masters)
Victories of the Saints: Stories from Church History (Cleaver)
  Later edition, 1875
A History of the Holy Eastern Church. Part I: General Introduction. In 2 vols. (Masters, Parker)

1851

The Followers of the Lord: Stories from Church History (Masters)
  3rd edition, 1871; reprinted by S.P.C.K., 1905
Mediaeval Hymns and Sequences
  3rd Edition, 1867
Hymni Ecclesiae (Parker)
Hymnal Noted: Part I (Novello)
A Short Commentary on the Hymnal Noted from Ancient Sources intended chiefly for the Use of the Poor (Masters)
Joy and Gladness: A Christmas Carol (Masters)
A History of the Holy Eastern Church: Appendix containing lists of the Sees (Masters)
Lectures on Church Difficulties of the Present Time (Cleaver)
  New edition with introduction by W. J. E. Bennett, 1871

1852

The Bible and the Bible only. A lecture (Masters)
  Reprinted in *Occasional Sermons*, 1873
Evenings at Sackville College: Legends for Children (Masters)
  Reprinted by S.P.C.K., 1909
Sequentiae ex Missalibus (Parker)
Pictorial Crucifixes: By a Priest of the Diocese (Masters)
Mammon: A Seatonian Prize Poem (Cambridge)

1853

A History of the Church for the use of Children. Part I (Masters). This part reaches the Council of Chalcedon. Three volumes were intended.
  Reprinted by A. R. Mowbray & Co., 1903
Bunyan's Pilgrim's Progress for the Use of Children in the English Church (Parker)
A Statement of the Late Proceedings of the Lord Bishop of Chichester against the Warden of Sackville College (Masters)
Carols for Christmastide (Novello)

1854

Carols for Eastertide (Novello)
Hymnal Noted: Part II (Novello)
Hymnal Noted with Scriptural References (Novello)
Confession and Absolution. A lecture (Masters)
Sermon for Proposed New Church in Liverpool
Readings for the Aged: 2nd Series (Masters)
The Egyptian Wanderers: A Story for Children of the Great Tenth Persecution
    Reprinted by S.P.C.K., 1903
The Warnings of Christmas Eve: Two Sermons (Masters)
The Farm of Aptonga: A Story of the Times of St Cyprian (Cleaver)
    Reprinted by S.P.C.K., 1902

1855

The Railway Accident: Tales for Young Men and Women (Parker)
The Ancient Liturgies of the Gallican Church, with an Introductory Dissertation.
    Edited by J. M. Neale and G. H. Forbes (Burntisland)
Lent Legends: Stories from Church History (Masters)
    3rd edition, 1884; repr. S.P.C.K., 1905

1856

The Life and Times of Patrick Torry, D.D., with an Appendix on the Scottish Liturgy (Masters)
Epistola Critica de Sequentiis (Daniel's *Thesaurus Hymnologia*, Tom. 5) (Leipsic: J. T. Loeschke)
A Handbook for Travellers in Portugal (J. Murray). Rose Macaulay wrote of this: "It is one of the best that exists, and ran into many editions; every wise traveller to Portugal has taken it with him ever since" (*They went to Portugal*, 1946, p. 209)
The Moral Concordances of St Antony of Padua (Hayes)
    4th edition; new edition, 1898
Mediaeval Preachers and Mediaeval Preaching (Mozley)
    New edition, 1873
Judith: A Seatonian Prize Poem (Cambridge)
Readings for the Aged: 3rd Series (Masters)
"Tractarian Delusions", Catholic Truth: An Answer to the Reverend E. B. Elliott (Masters)
A History of Sackville College (Masters)
The Two Huts: An Allegory (Masters)

1857

Tales on the Apostles' Creed (Masters)
    Reprinted by S.P.C.K., 1907
The Lewes Riot, its Causes and Consequences: A Letter to the Bishop of Chichester (Masters)

1857

Theodora Phranza, reprinted from the *Churchman's Companion,* 1853–4 (Masters)
   Reprinted by S.P.C.K., 1903; translated into Romaic (Modern Greek), 1860
The Hours of our Lord's Passion, translated from the Latin (Masters)
The Litany of the Holy Name, translated from the Latin (Masters)
Sinai: A Seatonian Prize Poem (Cambridge)

1858

A History of the so-called Jansenist Church of Holland (Parker)
Sermons on the Canticles (Painter)
Readings for the Aged: 4th Series (Masters)
Egypt: Two Seatonian Prize Poems (Cambridge)
Gill's Lap (reprinted from the *Penny Post* of 1857) (Parker)

1859

The Rhythm of Bernard de Morlaix on the Celestial Country (Hayes)
   Eight editions; reprinted by S.P.C.K., 1911
The Lazar House of Leros: A Tale of the Eastern Church in the Seventeenth Century (Parker)
   Reprinted by S.P.C.K.
The Lily of Tiflis
   Reprinted by S.P.C.K.
The Lions of Wady-Araba
   Reprinted by S.P.C.K.
"He said, Come." *A sermon preached at the Dedication Festival of St Matthias, Stoke Newington, 30 June 1859*
The Disciples at Emmaus: A Seatonian Prize Poem (Cambridge)
Greek Liturgies of SS. Mark, James, Clement, Chrysostom, and Basil (Hayes)
   2nd edition, 1868
English Translation of Greek Liturgies (Hayes)
   2nd edition, revised by R. F. Littledale, 1869, with title *Translations of the Primitive Liturgies*
Sunday Afternoons at an Orphanage (Masters)
   2nd edition, 1869
Voices from the East: Documents on the present state and working of the Oriental Church (Masters)

1860

The Sea Tigers
   Reprinted by S.P.C.K.
Ruth: A Seatonian Prize Poem (Cambridge)
A Commentary on the Psalms. Vol. I (Masters)
The Christian Nurse. Translated from the French of Gautrelet. Edited by J. M. Neale (Hayes)
The 29th Canon, and Reasons for its Abrogation: A Letter to the Bishop of Oxford (Masters)

1861

Text Emblems: Twelve beautiful designs, engraved by Dalziel, illustrating the Mystical Interpretation of as many verses from the Old Testament (Hayes)
    2nd edition, 1877

Additional Reasons for the Abrogation of the 29th Canon: A Second Letter to the Bishop of Oxford (Masters)

The History of the Council of Florence. Translated from the Russian by Basil Popoff. Edited by J. M. Neale (Masters)

1862

Notes on Dalmatia, Croatia, Istria, Styria, with a Visit to Montenegro (Hayes)

An Earnest Plea for the Retention of the Scotch Liturgy: A Letter to the Bishop of Brechin (Masters)
    Reprinted 1873

King Josiah: A Seatonian Prize Poem (Cambridge)

Hymns of the Eastern Church (Hayes)

1863

Essays in Liturgiology and Church History (Saunders, Otley & Co.). A collection of essays which appeared in *The Christian Remembrancer*

The Seven Churches of Asia: A Seatonian Prize Poem (Cambridge)

1864

Seatonian Prize Poems (Masters). Eleven poems, collected

1865

Extreme Men: A Letter to A. J. Beresford Hope, Esq. (Masters)

Hymns, chiefly Mediaeval, on the Joys and Glories of Paradise (Hayes)

Sisterhoods of the Church of England. A lecture

1866

Hymns for use during the Cattle Plague (Novello, S.P.C.K.)

Stabat Mater Speciosa, by Jacopone da Todi. In Latin and English (Hayes)

POSTHUMOUS PUBLICATIONS

1867

Hymns suitable for Invalids. Selected by the Rev. R. F. Littledale (Hayes)

Sermons for Children. Edited by the Rev. J. S. Haskoll (Hayes)
    3rd edition, 1872; new editions 1897 and 1913

Sermons on the Song of Songs (a reprint with additions, of *Sermons on the Canticles*). Edited by J.H. (Hayes)

1868

Sermons for the Minor Festivals (a reprint, with additions, of *Readings for the Aged,* Vol. II; forming Vol. IV of *Sackville College Sermons*) (Masters)

1868

Commentary on the Psalms, Vols. I and II (Masters) Neale's work went up to Psalm 59 in Vol. II. The work was completed by the Rev. R. F. Littledale with two further volumes to cover the whole Psalter. There have been several later editions of the whole work

    Fr Hebert makes the following observation on a part of this work: "The Essay by J. M. Neale entitled 'Dissertation on the Mystical and Literal Interpretation of the Psalms' . . . Vol. I, pp. 414–58, deserves to be called a classic."

He adds that the defect is that the exegesis lacks "the needed discipline of a critical theology" (A. G. Hebert, *The Throne of David,* 1941).

Revision of the Lectionary: A Letter to Bishop Hamilton of Salisbury (a fragment begun shortly before the author's last illness, and never completed). Edited by J.H. (Hayes)

The Virgin's Lamp. Prayers and Devout Exercises for English Sisters, chiefly selected by J. M. Neale (Wakeling, Rivingtons)

1869

Catechetical Notes and Class Questions (Hayes)

Sermons Preached in a Religious House, 1st Series, 2 Vols. Edited by J.H. (Masters)

Via Fidelium. Litanies, Stations, and Hours, chiefly translated by J. M. Neale (Wakeling, Hayes)

Sermons on Passages of the Psalms (Hayes)

1870

The Night Hours of the Church (Breviary Night Offices). Vols. I and II, partly translated by J. M. N. (Hayes)

Sermons on the Blessed Sacrament (Wakeling, Hayes)
        7 editions; new edition, 1914

1871

The Census. A sermon preached in the chapel of Sackville College on the Census Sunday, 1861 (Masters)

Sermons on the Apocalypse, the Holy Name, and the Proverbs (Hayes)

Sermons Preached in Sackville College Chapel, Vol. I, *Advent to Whitsuntide* (a reprint, with large additions, of *Readings for the Aged*) (Masters)

1872

Sermons Preached in Sackville College Chapel, Vol. II, *Trinity*

1873

Sermons Preached in Sackville College Chapel, Vol. III, *Lent and Passiontide*

Occasional Sermons preached in Various Churches (Hayes)

A History of the Holy Eastern Church: The Patriarchate of Antioch. Completed by the Rev. G. Williams (Rivingtons)

1874

Sermons Preached in a Religious House, 2nd Series, 2 vols. (Masters)

1875

Sermons for some Feast Days (Hayes)

1876

Sermons for the Church Year, 2 vols. (Hayes)

1877

Sermons on Passages from the Prophets, 2 vols. (Hayes)
The Night Hours of the Church. Vol. III (Hayes)
Notes on the Divine Office (Hayes)

1878

Readings for the Aged. Selected from *Sermons in Sackville College,* by the Rev.
R. F. Littledale (Masters)

1884

Selections from the Writings of John Mason Neale (Rivingtons)

Index